# The Diary of a CFD Trader

How to make serious money from contracts for difference

Catherine Davey

HARRIMAN HOUSE LTD
3A Penns Road
Petersfield
Hampshire
GU32 2EW
GREAT BRITAIN

Tel: +44 (0)1730 233870
Fax: +44 (0)1730 233880
Email: enquiries@harriman-house.com
Website: www.harriman-house.com

First published in 2006 by Wrightbooks an imprint of John Wiley & Sons Australia,
Ltd 42 McDougall Street, Milton Qld 4064 under the title "Making money from CFD
trading: how I turned $13k into $30k in 3 months"

This edition published in Great Britain in 2009
Copyright © Catherine Davey 2006

The right of Catherine Davey to be identified as Author has been asserted
in accordance with the Copyright, Design and Patents Act 1988.

ISBN: 978-1-906659-06-6

British Library Cataloguing in Publication Data
A CIP catalogue record for this book can be obtained from the British Library.

Stock charts reproduced with permission from IT-Finance
Printed and bound by MPG Books Group

# Contents

# Preface to the 2009 edition

I originally wrote this book in 2006, when markets were booming and no one could see an end to the good times. It's now late 2008 and the financial markets – and indeed the global economy – are a very different place. However, over this period CFDs have gone from strength to strength, such that trading in them is expected to soon reach countries like the United States and Japan.

But trading of any kind – including CFDs – is not easy. I still believe trading is the most demanding endeavour you will ever undertake. When I was a futures broker I saw very successful lawyers, doctors, accountants and engineers try to become successful traders and fail. Profitable trading, especially the achievement of long-term consistent profits, requires a vastly different skill-set from most other careers. The rules that apply to succeeding in most normal careers – hard work, good customer service, clever marketing, smart networking – are all useless in trading.

Writing this book added an extra pressure to my trading because I knew that the motivations and results would be made public. With hindsight I realise the profit I made was despite myself, not because of any great trading talents. These will become obvious as you read the book because I have done my best to highlight the errors of my ways and offer smarter alternatives. Above all, you will notice I lacked discipline and consistency. This should be some comfort for new CFD traders because these two skills are not something God-given, but can be easily nurtured.

Finally, I'd like to offer a new piece of advice: do whatever it takes to 'de-emotionalise' your trading. The highs of trading success will always be more than cancelled out by the lows when you are not trading from a rock-solid foundation of objective market knowledge and confidence. Having interviewed many experienced traders over the years as a journalist, the common factor of unsuccessful (and unhappy) traders is an inability to divorce who they are from the trades they make. This book is a working example of my own journey to rise above that common affliction.

## For non-Australian readers

When I wrote this book I was mainly trading Australian stocks and so these are the trades that I mention here. However, all my trades were driven by technical analysis (not specific to the Australian market), and the trading lessons learnt are equally applicable to CFDs trading in any market.

Note: Charts of the companies I traded can be found at http://au.finance.yahoo.com (although not all the companies still exist).

Catherine Davey

Sydney, 2008

# Preface to the 2006 edition

I wrote my first book, *Contracts for Difference: Master the Trading Revolution*, in 2003. I had stumbled upon contracts for difference, or 'CFDs', when I was writing a story for Australian financial website InvestorWeb in 2002. Back then CFDs were virtually unknown in Australia and attracted no media attention. Less than a year later, my book had hit the stores and the revolution was well on its way. Now CFDs are the hot new product for private traders, with a fan club from every corner of the trading and investing world, including former futures traders, hedge fund managers and of course traditional share traders. When I started writing my first book there were just two CFD providers in Australia; now there are around half-a-dozen, and the number has continued to grow during the time it has taken me to write this book.

My dream had always been eventually to trade for a living. CFDs made that goal seem much more attractive and easier to attain.

I joined the swelling ranks of CFD traders in 2004, paring back my freelance commitments so that I could realise my ambition. I quickly discovered that the difference between writing about CFDs and actually trading them was significant. Having spent six years working as the in-house technical analyst for InvestorWeb, I had considered myself a competent market commentator and analyst. At different times in my career I had traded shares and other derivative products, admittedly with mostly limited success, but I believed I had accumulated enough experience to avoid some of the pitfalls the average trader faces. I was wrong. Not only did I have to negotiate all the old traps again, but I also had to become familiar with the unique aspects of CFD trading.

The core of this book is a trading diary I kept over a three-month period in 2005, trading CFDs full time. Between the end of June and the end of September, I turned $13,000 into more than $30,000, but it was not easy. My path to success was not simple, nor straight, and I did not hit the ground running. Before I started writing this book I was in a losing cycle, which continued as the first weeks passed. I made many obvious mistakes from the outset and continued to make many of these same mistakes as the book progressed. There was one point at which I thought seriously about giving up on both trading and writing the book. I spent time crying on the shoulders of friends and family. I questioned my ability to trade and my self-esteem took a battering. I think these feelings are common to all traders.

It has been my aim to provide a book that not only describes a practical means of potentially making money from CFDs, but also presents an honest discussion of the emotional journey. I am hoping my honesty will comfort and inspire anyone going through the inevitable emotional downside we all encounter at some stage and with a certain amount of regularity, in our trading. I hope, too, that the positive lessons I have learnt will inspire you.

Catherine Davey

Sydney, 2006

# Introduction

## What are CFDs?

Contracts for difference, or 'CFDs', are a derivative trading instrument – their value is derived from or determined by the price of a stock being traded on a market. When you enter into a contract for difference with a provider, you are in effect taking a bet on a stock's future price action. You enter a contract or 'open a position' when a particular stock is trading at a specific price; the CFD provider agrees that when you close the position, terminating the contract, it will pay you the difference between the stock's starting price and the price it is currently trading at.

For example, if the price of Telstra shares is quoted on the Australian Stock Exchange (ASX) at $4.35, a Telstra share CFD will be quoted at the same price. If you buy 100 Telstra share CFDs at this price, and Telstra shares subsequently trade at $4.40, you can close the position and take a profit of $5 – the difference between the underlying shares' initial value of $435 and their subsequent value of $440. If, on the other hand, the price the shares are trading at falls to $4.30, and you close the position, you will lose $5. You don't own shares in Telstra at any point in this scenario: you are only speculating on their price movement. CFDs mirror the price of shares, allowing traders to take advantage of share price movements without actually owning physical shares.

## Why CFDs?

I was first attracted to the idea of trading CFDs because, unlike other derivative instruments available, their price action is exactly like the price action of their underlying product. As a technical analyst, making trading decisions on the basis of chart patterns, I saw benefits in being able to scan the charts of the underlying share and use the information gleaned there to trade the CFD, knowing that their price movements would be identical. From a price perspective, CFDs and shares were the same, but for my purposes CFDs were better. Unlike options or warrants, they would allow me to get set in a market that had no expiry date and traded no premium.

I had spent years analysing shares for InvestorWeb. As a former futures broker and trader, I thought the share market seemed a much gentler and easier market to trade. While a futures market such as pork bellies or coffee can go through the equivalent of a stock market crash and recovery in a few hours, share prices are like the country cousin, moving relatively slowly. CFDs would allow me to trade the gentle world of shares and get the same bang for my buck that a futures market would provide. The bang would be supplied by leverage – in my opinion, CFDs' greatest advantage. With limited funds – in my case, just $13,000 – extraordinary gains can be accumulated. Leverage is the launching pad that can turn a sometime investor into a full-scale trader. To understand the miraculous power of leverage consider this: during the time I kept my trading diary, the S&P/ASX 200 increased around 9.6%, which isn't bad if you annualise it to 38%, but in that same three-month period my account balance grew over 132%. Annualise that figure and it becomes ridiculous!

CFD trading also attracts low brokerage charges. With my CFD provider I can enter a trade for as little as $10. This makes CFDs a very powerful learning tool. Small trades with low brokerage allow new traders the opportunity to get their feet wet without getting killed with commissions. As little as one share can be traded at a time. It might seem ludicrous to start so small, but if you've never traded before, the process of trading just one share gives you the same feelings as trading a more realistically sized order: it is an opportunity to practise trading discipline without the risks and stress of larger exposure to the market.

Another key advantage of CFDs is that they can be traded profitably even when the market is going down. One of the big problems with traditional share investing for me has always been the difficulty in making money when the market is falling. With its focus on positive price growth, old school share trading is only half the story. My futures background has taught me that a falling market is often as good and sometimes an even better money-making opportunity than a rising market. It is the ability to profit from a fall in prices that separates traders from investors, and CFDs make this very easy. The market will periodically enter a downturn and eventually there will be a long-term correction. Both of these events are potentially profitable for CFD traders.

## Why a trading diary?

Trading for a living is different from running any other kind of small business. There are no customers to entice, no products to sell. Instead, trading is a relationship between you and the market. Like any relationship, its success depends upon the effort and respect you give it. Once you've been in the trading game for a while, you'll start to notice how frequently educators and successful traders talk about the importance of keeping a trading diary. Writing in diary form allows you to describe not just the actual trades you take, but also how you feel and the measures you employ to succeed in the trading process. Trading is not just a matter of making or losing money: your emotional reaction to each loss and win perpetuates your trading success or failure.

As I updated my own diary over the three-month period, I was able to see the benefits of this practice directly. It not only forced me to investigate my emotional response to trading, but also showed me the logical and sometimes illogical reasons I had for taking trades. I would normally describe my trading as intuition-driven and haphazard, but keeping a trading diary revealed that there was method in my madness and helped me crystallise my approach.

The diary forced me to look for reasons for victory or defeat, when usually I would simply move on without introspection or self-analysis. Until I started to keep a record, I had no idea how often I would repeat my mistakes and contradict myself, or how easy it was for me to slip into bad habits. I am hoping that by exposing my frailties as a trader, I will help you feel less alone and empower you to confront your own weaknesses.

I have shared moments in the diary that, in retrospect, were extremely personal and made me feel vulnerable. My ability to share such moments makes me glad to be a woman, because talking about feelings and confessing flaws seems to come easier for us. However, the emotional processes that are part of the trading journey are the same for both sexes. The cycle of success, loss, fear, desperation, hope and hopelessness does not discriminate between men and women. My aim has been to provide all readers with ideas to help them deal with this inevitable cycle.

A final, and probably the most important, reason I had for keeping this diary was to bring some credibility to trading as an occupation. Big claims and spectacular gains are so commonplace in the investment and trading world that it makes the whole business seem dubious. This is partly due to the number of authors and educators in the field who do not trade. I met plenty as a futures broker: some of the highest profile commentators in Australia were also some of the worst traders on our books. The diary format offered me the opportunity to 'walk the talk'– to offer a truthful and realistic picture of making money from trading.

## The characters in this book

Although my trading diary provides the central focus of this book, I am not the only character in this story. I trade from my home office in an eastern Sydney beachside suburb, and my daytime companion is my small dog. One of my flatmates is also home sometimes during the day, and he occasionally comes to talk to me about the garden, among other topics. I am not always interested in the rockery he has built, especially when the market is very volatile. He's a former institutional and private trader, so he understands that sometimes the market is too busy for me to talk about the pansies. If you are trying to trade from home it is important to set these sorts of boundaries with family.

Throughout the period in which I was keeping my diary, I was lucky enough to have access to the director of a CFD provider. I have included my actual conversations with him and the advice he gave me in this book. I didn't always agree with him, and sometimes did directly the opposite of his recommendation, but his thoughts on the market are always worth considering – he has been both an institutional and independent trader, and has been involved in CFDs since they were introduced in the UK in 1999. He is referred to as The Director.

Other characters in the book include David L, an analyst and commentator, and Ashley J, a trading educator and coach. David L and I exchanged ideas on the market on a daily basis. Again, we disagreed plenty of times, but his input was still valuable.

You will discover some other recurring characters, but I don't want to spoil the surprise.

## How to use this book

I have structured this book to allow you to follow the action in my trading diary and learn as you go. Each day's diary entry begins with a figure representing the balance of my account as it appears on my broker's statement. It varies from day to day, fluctuating as I close existing positions and enter new ones, and as the prices of the CFDs I trade move up and down. At first all my trades are on the local market, but after a while you will see a second figure appear: this is the running profit and loss of my US dollar exposure.

Each week of trading is contained within a separate chapter. At the end of each chapter you will find a cumulative profit and loss total. This is based purely on positions I have closed out, and brokerage and interest charges have been deducted. Underneath the weekly profit and loss you will find a list of my trading statistics, including my biggest winning trade of the week, the biggest loser, my win/loss ratio and a summary of my performance during the week.

The diary entries for the week are followed by sections called 'What have I learnt?' and 'Do's and don'ts'. In these sections I share my thoughts on my performance during the week and my strengths and weaknesses, identifying the lessons I have learnt that I can pass on to readers. Unfortunately, mistakes I made were often repeated, as I didn't necessarily learn from them myself, but I hope you will benefit from my experience.

Following the diary entries for each week is a section called 'Lingo and lessons', in which I explain new terminology and trader's jargon, offer observations I've made during the course of the week and elaborate on important points that I felt the reader should understand.

After the lingo and lessons in each chapter, you will find a trading tip – a repeatable entry or exit strategy based on important practical insights I have gained through observation of the market and trading during the week. The trading tip section includes a chart or diagram for an easy visual reference.

I assume that readers have a basic knowledge of the sharemarket, and are familiar with trading jargon, but where I thought it might be necessary to introduce a new term, I have added a definition to the 'Lingo and lessons' section at the end of each week's diary entries. New words which appear in the lingo section are bolded when they first appear in the text.

I also assume that the reader is familiar with the basic concepts of technical analysis, and knows how to read a candlestick chart, showing a stock's price action. If you need further information about technical analysis, try John J. Murphy's bible, *Technical Analysis of the Financial Markets* (Prentice Hall Press, 1999). For an introduction to reading candlesticks, I'd recommend Louise Bedford's *The Secret of Candlestick Charting* (Wrightbooks, 2000).

This book concludes with a graph of my performance relative to the S&P/ASX 200 – the standard investment management benchmark. This graph provides insight into the day-to-day volatility of my profit and loss, as well as a realistic point of comparison with the market index.

An important development since my last book was published has been a spectacular resumption of the bull market for Australian shares. My trading diary was written during this period of strong growth, and this has obviously given the book a bullish bias: I have gone long on CFDs more often than I have gone short. I believe a raging uptrend can give new CFDs traders an unrealistic opinion of their trading ability. Preserving profits from profitable positions when there is a correction and making money from falls in the market are just as important as exploiting the upside. I made regular attempts to make money from a falling market with varying success; however, given the market's upward bias, the downside probably didn't receive the attention it deserved on a day-to-day basis. To address this, I have included a discussion about making money from the downside in the last chapter.

I am glad to have been involved with CFDs almost since their inception in this country. My first book had a theoretical approach; I am hoping that this book will provide traders with practical and realistic steps they can follow in order to trade CFDs successfully.

# Getting started

In this preliminary chapter, I will explain some basic concepts and then outline my trading approach. If you are already an experienced trader, comfortable with sharemarket jargon, you can probably skip over the basic concepts and go straight to the details about my trading method.

## Market jargon

Feedback from showing early drafts of this book to peers indicated that I used a lot of market jargon. Working on dealing desks and as a broker means the jargon has become second nature to me. For the average private trader, it's not always obvious what the jargon means, so I have added this section here at the beginning of the book to lay a foundation of terms commonly used throughout.

### Long or short/bull or bear

If you've ever traded shares, you are probably familiar with the terms 'bull' and 'bear', but you won't necessarily be familiar with the idea of 'going long' or 'going short'. Most share investors aim to buy and hold and then sell at a profit when the market goes up. With CFDs, you can make money from prices going up, but you can also make money when prices go down. If you think the market is going up, you're a bull, and you are likely to take a long position. If you think the market is going down, you're a bear, and you're likely to take a short position.

Going long means entering a position by buying something and then selling it when the price has risen. Going short means entering a position by selling something you don't actually own, and buying it back when the price has fallen.

Just say the price of BlueScope Steel (BSL) is quoted as $8.35-$8.36. If I expect the price to rise, I will go long by buying at the offer price of $8.36. This gives me a long position. I will make money if I exit the position by selling at a price above $8.36. If I expect the price to fall, I will go short by selling at the bid price of $8.35. This will give me a 'short position'. I will make money if I exit the position by buying at a price below my entry at $8.35.

Some people have a bent for the upside or the downside – you're either a natural bull or natural bear. I'm a natural bear, so I find it hard not to go short no matter how bullish the market is.

A benefit of going short CFDs is that you will be paid interest on the position. If you have a long position, you have all the benefits that someone holding physical shares enjoys, such as dividends, although you do not receive voting rights.

If you have trouble with the concept of going short, don't feel bad – it does seem strange at first. I spent half an hour with one of my flatmates trying to explain the idea of selling something you don't own, and he's a doctor!

## Margin and leverage

CFDs are a unique way of trading share price action, requiring only a fraction of the capital you would need to trade physical shares. The amount of cash you must deposit as margin varies from one CFD provider to another, but the going rate is usually somewhere between 3% and 20% of the value of the underlying shares. For instance, to trade a position worth $20,000 with 5% margin requirement, you will need a deposit of $1000. This equates to 20 times leverage.

## Order book, market depth or price depth/bids and offers

When people refer to the 'order book', they are referring to all current buy and sell orders for a particular stock. These can be viewed on a 'market depth' or 'price depth' information screen. Your market depth screen will usually set out all buy orders for a stock, ranked in order from highest bid to lowest. It will also show you all sell orders, ranked from lowest offer to highest.

The 'bid price' is the best or highest price market participants are prepared to pay for a stock. The 'offer price' is the best or lowest price at which market participants are prepared to sell a stock. The screen shot below shows price depth for BlueScope Steel. The bid price is $8.35. The offer price is $8.36.

**Figure 1. Bids and offers on the price depth screen**

| Price Depth BSL (Au) | | | |
|---|---|---|---|
| 9,274 | **8.350** / | **8.360** | 208 |
| 9,515 | 8.340 | 8.370 | 3,000 |
| 9,160 | 8.330 | 8.380 | 2,900 |
| 12,025 | 8.320 | 8.390 | 16,882 |
| 5,500 | 8.310 | 8.400 | 25,000 |
| 27,040 | 8.300 | 8.410 | 2,000 |
| 20,189 | 8.290 | 8.420 | 6,500 |
| 300 | 8.280 | 8.430 | 15,983 |
| 1,360 | 8.270 | 8.440 | 2,000 |
| 5,659 | 8.260 | 8.450 | 4,100 |

| | | | | | |
|---|---|---|---|---|---|
| Mid | 8.3550 | Change | -0.0300 | High | 8.380 |
| Open | 8.3450 | % Chg. | -0.36% | Low | 8.340 |
| Close | 8.3850 | | | | |

© IT-Finance

## Volume and liquidity

Looking back at the price depth screen on the previous page, you will see that a column of smaller numbers runs beside the central columns that list the bids and offers. These smaller numbers represent the 'volume' – that is, the number of shares – which traders wish to buy or sell at each particular price. The number on the left-hand side of the bid price represents the volume traders wish to buy at that bid price. The number on the right-hand side of the offer price represents the volume traders wish to sell at that offer price. Our sample screenshot shows us that market participants want to buy 9274 share CFDs at the bid price of $8.35, and to sell 208 share CFDs at $8.36.

I consider market depth when deciding if a stock is looking strong or weak. Large numbers of orders at prices only incrementally below the best bid price indicate that the market is 'well bid'; that is, likely to be strong. Similarly, large numbers of sell orders at prices incrementally above the best offer price also indicate that the market is likely to be strong. However, this is not always the case: the order book can change quickly, and orders can be removed suddenly and at any time during the trading session.

Liquidity is shown in the number of orders and the volume of shares at each price level. High liquidity means there are many orders and large volume. Low liquidity means there is lower volume and/or few orders placed in the market.

## Order types

Before you start trading, you need to know your order types so that you can use them to maximum advantage. The following is only a brief introduction; for more detail, please see my first book, *Contracts for Difference: Master the Trading Revolution* (Wrightbooks, 2003).

**Market order** – Entering on a market order means accepting the current bid price to go short or buying at the current offer price to go long. Market orders are used by traders who are eager to take a position immediately and are not interested in waiting for the price to go lower before buying or for it to rise before selling. For example, if BSL is quoted at $8.35-$8.36, to buy 'at market' would be to pay the current offer price of $8.36. To sell at market is to enter at the current bid price of $8.35. Nine times out of ten I will enter on a market order.

**Limit order** – A limit order is placed below the current market level for a buy order and above it for a sell order. A limit can be used to enter or exit a trade. If traders want to pay less than the current offer to buy, or sell at a price higher than the current bid price, they'll place a limit order. For example, if BSL is quoted at $8.35-$8.36, traders may want to wait, hoping that they will be able to buy at a price lower than $8.36. Therefore they might place an order to buy 'on limit' at $8.30.

**Stop-loss order** – In my trading diary, I will often note that I have been 'stopped out' of a position. This means my CFD provider closes my position because a stock's price has hit the level at which I have placed a stop-loss order. A stop-loss order is placed below the market for a long position and above the market for a short position, with the aim of limiting losses should the position go against you. Stop-loss orders do not only apply to losing positions; they can also be used to exit a winning position and realise profits.

**Trailing stop-loss orders** – To 'trail' a stop-loss order is to move the order closer to the current price in order to maximise profits or minimise losses from an open position. Setting a trailing stop is common practice when a position moves into profit and the market continues to move in the direction of the profitable trade. As a position becomes more profitable, I continue to trail my stop-loss level. Well, that's the theory. Your CFD provider will not trail a stop-loss order automatically. You must do this for yourself.

'One cancels other' order – If you have a clear target for a profitable exit, you might want to work a limit order in conjunction with a stop-loss order. This can be done with an order called 'one cancels other' (OCO). As soon as one 'leg' of the order is executed, the other side is immediately cancelled. An OCO is commonly used to simultaneously work orders to exit an existing position if it goes into loss, or to exit if it is in sufficient profit.

'If done' order – The 'if done' order is another contingent order that is handy if you are not able to watch price. If you are entering on a limit order, the 'if done' order can be attached to a stop-loss order, making sure that as soon as your entry is executed, you have a protective stop in place.

## Support and resistance

Support levels and resistance levels are probably the most basic concepts of technical analysis, and they are the two most important tools of my trading strategy. A stock's support level is based on old chart lows. It is the point below the current price action at which downward price movement has halted in the past. A stock's resistance level is based on old chart highs, and is the point above the current price action at which upward price movement has previously halted. Support and resistance 'lines' can be plotted on a chart.

Looking at Figure 2, it is obvious that a support level, once breached to the downside, can become resistance, and vice versa.

Even if you use a trading system based on more advanced indicators, you should still be aware of support and resistance levels on a stock's chart. I am always looking for old chart reversal levels, and stay extra vigilant when prices get near these levels. If a support or resistance

BID - Buy - THEY
I sell
8-50

THEY
SELL OFFER
I Buy
8-35

MARKET
DEPTH - VOLUME ON BOARD

LARGE Numbers Incrementally below best
Bid Price - Well Bid

Similarly Offer Prices Incrementally in No's
above Offer Price indicate likely strong Match

Limit Buy = Below Offer for me to buy
" Sell = Above Best for " " sell
    - To Enter or Exit

Stop Loss - Bid - above to Limit Loss or short

  "    "  OFFER = Below for Long

If done    | To Close
Contingent order | p 5
to protect | p 6 Support Res.

If market has no reaction to support
Resist = Strong Trend

Traders stress importance of Keeping Diary which should include the obvious + feelings (emotions) reasons! The successful ones. You have to take into account emotional impare, not just about money Reason for victory or defeat.

Some of the highest Profile Traders were also the biggest losers.

Candlesticks - against Team.                    COTTON
                                                WOOL

* Protecting Profits is Just as Important as Preservation Capital
ie. Market Correction SCALING p 142

MARKET DEPTH SCREEN - usually all Buy Orders ranked in order from highest to lowest it will also show SELL Orders from lowest to highest.
Screen Left - Buy Volume - Screen Right - Sell Orders
Pay attention to these Volume Nos

High Liquidity — Large Vol., Plent Orders.
Low      "      — Low Volume & Few Orders
C(A)O's require Tracking Stop Loss - Not Automatic.
Say on % you have to do yourself
One cancels the other, Safety order to ensure
Say Limit & Stop are both closed/cancelled on closure
If Done Order - Entry say on Limit ensure
a Stop Order is put in place as well.
* If a Support/Res. can Pause/stop a Trend its Important
* "  " .Market Swings Sup/Res. Off Trend has underlying strength
Book - The Secret of Candlestick Charting
Louise Bedford (Wright books, 2000

level can pause or stop a trend it is important; if a market shrugs it off, it says that trend has underlying strength.

**Figure 2. Support and resistance**

© IT-Finance

## Double bottoms and double tops

A double top pattern is a twice-tested high that is confirmed when the intervening low is breached on a closing basis. A double bottom is a twice-tested low that is confirmed when the intervening high between the two lows is breached on a closing basis.

A double bottom, especially in a bull market, is one of the most consistently reliable patterns. This pattern not only gives a safe buy signal, but usually provides an early buy signal, too, because the pattern is often the starting point for gains far greater than your initial pattern-based targets.

7

## Spike tops and bottoms

Spike tops and bottoms are another favourite pattern of mine. They usually represent extremes of emotions and as such are terminal points of overbought or oversold conditions. They form within the day and require a fast reaction to exploit the turnaround.

## Range

A stock's trading range is an important tool. Lots of my entry and exit signals are based on chart patterns that form when the price moves between resistance and support on several occasions, creating a rectangular pattern.

When a stock makes new lows and then starts trading within a relatively narrow price range without making new lows, this is called a basing range. Some stocks will often reverse into a sustainable new uptrend after the confirmation of such a pattern, while others will consistently make spike lows or rapid unchecked lows before resuming the uptrend.

'Consolidation' and 'congestion' are interchangeable terms which describe a trading range that does not result in a reversal in the trend. They are in effect a pause before the trend resumes and are equally important buy or sell signals.

## Continuation pattern

A continuation pattern is seen when price movements resume in the direction of a trend which was established before a trading range started to form.

## Intra-day break-outs

I also look at intra-day break-outs compared to closing levels. Rangebound or consolidation patterns often contain intra-day breaches of the range, but then close within the range. This is often a good buy signal in the case of a downside break and a good sell signal in the case of an upside break. I discuss this in the trading tip I present at the end of week 3.

# My trading platform

Many of the best features of CFD trading are related to the kind of internet-based trading platforms that are around today. The best brokers now provide their clients with software offering a range of services, including charting facilities, news and online order placement. Having spent years executing futures orders by telephone, I believe this kind of facility makes my trading more disciplined, results in far fewer errors and saves me much of the stress and time involved in talking to a broker.

I use a market-market CFD platform that gives me flexibility in placing orders, along with instant access to the market and real-time profit and loss statements.

I have a series of prices for share and index CFDs loaded on my CFD trading platform.

The platform has a position-keeping log and pending order log, both of which are called 'blotters'. I always keep both blotters open. This reminds me to place stop-loss orders for open positions at my predetermined price levels. It also alerts me when these orders are potentially ready to be executed – when a price trades near my predetermined level, this is highlighted on my pending order blotter. The position-keeping blotter is useful because it shows 'tick-by-tick' or incremental changes in a continuously updated running profit and loss.

The platform also allows me to build a favourites list of individual share CFDs. I remove a stock from this list if I have a bad run of trades on it and decide I should stop trading it. This takes away the temptation.

My CFD platform also offers a world of other trading opportunities aside from local share CFDs – an entry into sophisticated markets that are usually only open to traders who maintain separate accounts to trade foreign exchange or futures. I can access and trade real-time markets such as oil, gold, silver, wheat, overseas share CFDs and index CFDs, US and euro treasury bonds, every major currency, many minor ones and cross rates. Whichever market I choose, my trading platform gives me access to charting facilities, market depth information (where available), and also gives me the ability to 'back-test' trading systems.

The back-testing facility on my trading platform allows any technical indicator to be tested using historical data. This opens up a range of possibilities for new traders looking to devise a tradable system. I would recommend using the back-testing facility on a number of different stocks. You might find some systems work best using weekly charts rather than daily charts, or give better signals about some stocks than others. The best approach can only be determined by a process of trial and error. You will also find there is a difference between the results you get when you back-test a system and the outcomes you achieve using it in real life.

## My trading method

Once you begin trading you will quickly discover there is no holy grail. The smartest way to make money is the way that suits you best, but you won't discover what this is until you start trading. The right approach will depend on your circumstances – whether you have a full-time job, how much time you can spend watching the screen, your financial means, and your actual analysis style. There is no single ideal approach, and developing your own trading style is a process of evolution.

I had my first trade back in the 1990s trading a US 30-year T-Bond futures contract on a joint account with my boyfriend at the time and another friend. The position was fabulously profitable at first, but then it turned down. We hung in there, but eventually took away only a meagre profit. That was the starting point of my trading education.

Like many trading neophytes, I studied the most complicated and esoteric strategies first. Gann, Elliott wave and astrology were some of the methods I subscribed to in my early days. They all worked, but each of them required an enormous amount of study and that made trading unenjoyable. Scouring an astronomical almanac for 'moon void of course' or 'Venus opposition Mars' was too laborious when all along I had the best trading tool staring me right in the face: pure price action on the chart. It took me years to realise just how important price was.

Acknowledging the importance of price led me to develop a trading approach that relies on some embarrassingly simple technical patterns.

I consider myself a 'break-out trader', that is, I buy stock once its price moves above a certain predetermined level and sell it when it drops below a certain level. I nearly always enter on a market order, which means that I pay the current offer price or sell at the current bid price, but I use a stop-loss order to exit. I very rarely use limit orders to open or close a position.

I have no mechanical trading approach and use no technical indicators and I don't care about volume traded, only volume on market depth. I watch price action, study the charts and am not afraid to buy high and sell low; stop and reverse; or get stopped out and re-enter in same direction if the price action says I should.

I also like to add to positions. This is sometimes called 'pyramiding' or 'scaling-in', and it means investing more in a position as it moves into profit. For example, imagine that you buy Aristocrat Leisure (ALL) at $10 for 1000 share CFDs. Each 1¢ move up or down in the price of ALL equals $10 that you have gained or lost. If the price of ALL goes up to $10.20, you might therefore decide to buy another parcel of 1000 shares. Now that you have doubled your exposure, every 1¢ price move means $20 is added to or subtracted from your account. As a position moves further in my favour, I continue to add, so that each incremental move in the underlying delivers increasing profits.

My trading approach could be characterised as having three basic steps:

1. Buy or sell on a break-out to enter.

2. Exit on a pullback for a buy or rebound for a sell.

3. Add to positions as they move in my favour and trail stop aggressively as profits grow.

I describe the various chart-based techniques I use in planning my entry and exit strategies throughout this book. You will also find a specific trading tip at the end of each chapter.

## My stock selection criteria

I started trading a limited selection of share CFDs using an approach based on nothing more than trial and error. I first looked for stocks that obeyed the rules of technical analysis, forming familiar patterns and moving to target once the patterns were confirmed. I chose stocks which followed these rules to a degree that would allow me to implement strategies based on the pattern outlined above. My 'usual suspects' include Aristocrat Leisure (ALL), BlueScope Steel (BSL), Coles Myer (CML), Newcrest Mining (NCM), Excel Coal (EXL),

Oxiana (OXR) and Jubilee Mines (JBM). There is one other stock that I began trading for the first time halfway through the book. It ended up being my most profitably traded CFD, but I won't tell you what it is just yet.

These days I know more about stock selection than when I started. The first thing I consider now is the market depth. As I explained above, market depth is the volume of interest from buyers and sellers – the number of offers or bids being made – at various price levels. You will find that market depth information becomes increasingly important as you become more serious about your trading. I rarely place an order, especially on the stocks that are traded at relatively low volumes, without checking the number of bids or offers being made first. This tells me whether there is enough volume available to cover my order.

Different stocks suit different traders. The names I gave above should not be read as a list of the best or the only share CFDs to trade. Some of those I have mentioned go off the boil at times, or become too unpredictable to trade. I am constantly trying new shares. You will find that some share CFDs might have a clear 'set-up' or entry pattern only infrequently – occasionally they may be very profitable, but the rest of the time they should be left alone. A good rule when considering trading a new share CFD is to check its liquidity. Thin or illiquid stocks, no matter how attractive their price action, can be frustrating and costly to trade. That was one of the best lessons I learnt when choosing which share CFDs to trade.

Apart from high chart predictability and good liquidity, the other criterion I base stock selection on is volatility. I am impatient, so trading a stock that takes two weeks to move 10¢ is agonising. It is not only boring, but also not cost-efficient. Every time I buy and hold a CFD position overnight I attract a financing charge. As long as the stock does nothing, it is costing me money.

Back-testing is another useful tool in stock selection. In the final month of my three-month trading period, I back-tested a system on my CFD platform and started trading it on a demo account. (I will discuss this in detail in my diary entries for week 11.) As it was only a demo account, I did not trade real money, so even though I was successful, my 'profits' on this account are not included in my final total profit figure. It was a departure from my normal trading style, which is much less rigid. However, the success of my back-testing experiment proves there is no single way to make money. It also is great inspiration for those traders hoping to make the break from full-time work to full-time trading. The trading system was based on a low-maintenance, end-of-day approach – a perfect interim strategy for traders with limited time wanting to gain a feel for the market before giving up their day job.

## My daily routine

I trade from home. I work from my laptop, using an extra screen. On one screen I have charts and live prices and on the other I have my own Excel spreadsheet with the day's open and closed positions. I have broadband and cable television connected to the office. I watch bad daytime programming more often than I look at the business channel. The business channel is most helpful before the market opens, when it has a run-down of the US markets and a pre-market summary of the local market. As the morning progresses, the focus on other Asian bourses does not interest me, so I tend to switch over.

The first thing I look at when I turn on the trading platform in the morning is the price action of the Dow Jones Industrial Average, spot gold, and crude oil. I often review positions if I see a big drop in my profit figures during the day. It is common to see a large profit as the market opens and then a fall in this figure as the day progresses.

I watch the charts – the 5-minute and the 30-minute charts as well as the daily charts. Like most traders, I work backwards from longer term to shorter term, analysing the weekly charts first, then the daily charts. As the day progresses, I focus chiefly on the intra-day charts. However, in the last half-hour before the close I check the daily chart again, trying to see how the day is likely to end. Although I am a short-term trader, taking a position for a maximum period of a few days or weeks, I always monitor closing price action. Closing prices are a good indication of how a stock might open the next day. When a downward day closes with a big rally on its highs, it is often a sign that there will be more buying the next day. However, this is not always the case: the close gives a better indication of the future performance of some stocks than others.

When trading gets really boring I lie on the couch in my trading room and watch TV or I go outside to check out the sea, take a closer look at my garden or play with small dog. I generally don't do much – just watch the prices.

I never call my CFD broker if I can help it, but have the number programmed into my mobile phone for easy access in case I am away from my desk. When I'm out of the office I use my mobile data service, which supplies prices to my mobile phone.

* * *

Now that we've covered the basics, we're ready to get started.

# Week 1

## The first cut

## Day 1

Tuesday, 28 June
Total: $12,942

---

I saw the film *Wall Street* back in the late 1980s and became interested in trading. The Director tells me he too first acquired a taste for trading when he watched the film as a teenager, sitting in a shed in Kerry in his native Ireland. I suspect there are many traders who caught the trading bug that way, in the days when the most famous line from the trading world was, 'Greed, for want of a better word, is good.' The greed is good quote doesn't ring true for most traders, though. In fact, I think the majority would say greed is often their downfall. I have two other favourite quotes from the film. The first is another Gekko saying, 'Greed captures the essence of the evolutionary spirit.' I think greed, the compulsion to make money, motivates us to trade but then leads us to areas of ourselves that we wouldn't normally go to. I think this is the reason why so many traders fail and give up. Lessons you learn about making or losing money can be painful, but the personal lessons you learn sometimes hurt even more. My other favourite quote sums up this phenomenon: the good guy character Lou says, 'Man looks in the abyss – there's nothing staring back at him. At that moment, man finds his character, and that's what keeps him out of the abyss.' There are very few events in an average person's life that will take them to the abyss, but if you trade, I can guarantee this will happen, and if you persevere, you'll find your character.

It all sounds melodramatic, but until you actually start trading you can't understand the enormity of the emotional journey involved. Someone once told me the best traders do it for the self-discovery, not the money. I suppose it's something like that old saying, 'What matters is the journey, not the destination.'

Before I even start my journey, I have to answer an important question: how much should I deposit into my trading account? I ask The Director. 'In general terms, if you want a 20 to 30% return on your money, an account balance of $30,000 to $40,000 would be good,' he suggests. I had thought that average clients started with about $10,000 in their accounts. 'Yeah, about that,' The Director says, 'maybe a little higher, say $20,000.' I set up a new trading account with a fresh balance of $13,000. If you consider that every $1000 is really worth $20,000 or $30,000, because of leverage, it seems like a reasonable figure, and I should be able to make some money from it. I like the number 13.

My first trading day is a Tuesday. I start the morning by checking the local index (the S&P/ASX 200) and the Dow. The local index has not been tracking the recent huge losses on the Dow, which was down 166 points last Wednesday and a further 120 points on Thursday. I take this as a positive. When any market bucks a general trend or a major market or sector trend, it shows its own underlying strength. A large move down in the Dow that is not followed by an equivalent downward move in the local market means that local stocks have more ready buyers, at least in the short-term.

It's not just the relationship between the US stock market and the local stock market that works this way. If a particular stock doesn't move down with its market sector, this often indicates relative strength. For example, if there were a move down in, say, the Australian materials sector index (XMJ), but BlueScope Steel (BSL) stock managed to beat off general index bearishness and make a strong move higher, many market participants would interpret this as a demonstration of BSL's underlying bullishness. This is not always the case, though; sometimes it's a matter of a particular market or stock playing catch-up.

I enter long positions in two share CFDs, both based on a simple break of resistance, one on Aristocrat Leisure (ALL), which can behave like a bucking bull, and one on BlueScope Steel (BSL), one of my favourites. I jump straight into both of these positions. I don't have trouble **pulling the trigger**, but many new traders do. This is normal, and there are a number of things you can do to build confidence. The first is to make sure you aren't gambling. Without a commitment to a trading strategy or approach, your trades are random and therefore tend towards gambling. When you don't have a system you believe in or put on a trade without confidence, you will find pulling the trigger difficult. Committing to an approach you are comfortable with will make entering trades much easier.

I usually risk around $350 on a single trade. I always try to place my stop-loss order at the same time I place my opening trade, because this is when I'm most objective. It makes sense, because the position size is determined by the stop-loss level.

The general rule around the markets is not to risk more than 2% of your total capital per trade. Personally, I generally choose to risk a maximum of $350 per trade. This represents 2.7% of my trading account starting balance of $13,000. If my account balance drops below $13,000, I do not automatically reduce my risk amount. I might have ten trades open at once, risking $350 on each trade. The amount of dollars you have decided to risk per trade will determine the amount you can invest, and therefore the size of the position you can take.

For example, imagine that I want to trade ALL, and that I open a position when ALL is trading at $11.17. I decide that I should exit the position if the price falls below an old chart support level at $10.85, so this is where I place my stop-loss order. The difference between the entry point and the stop-loss point is 32¢. I divide $350 by 32 to get a total of 1093. This is the number of share CFDs I will trade. I round it down to 1000 for the sake of convenience. This approach ensures that I am always trading a position size that takes into account my stop-loss level, my account size and my maximum risk amount.

To summarise, the way I determine my position size is to:

1. identify the entry price

2. identify the appropriate stop-loss level

3. determine the difference between the entry price and my stop-loss level in cents

4. divide my ideal risk amount by this figure.

This tells me the number of share CFDs I should trade – that is, my ideal position size.

Some stocks are more volatile than others, so they need wider stops. If you place a stop too close to your entry level, you don't give the price enough room to move, and you'll find that you are stopped out before you've had a chance to make any gains. However, when you set a wide stop, you should reduce your position size accordingly, to limit the amount you can lose.

When I'm making a decision about how tight a stop should be, I look at a stock's liquidity and what I call charting predictability. I am comfortable taking a bigger position in BSL than some other stocks, for instance, because it tends to be less volatile and more liquid, and it trades more predictably. By this I mean that there are few **false break-outs** on BSL charts.

# Day 2

Wednesday, 29 June
Total: $13,145

---

Before I start the trading day I check the performance of the Dow overnight and recent action of the local index compared with the Dow. I'm looking for anomalies. The Dow and the local index sometimes trade in sympathy, but the Australian market often goes its own way, and this is the case right now. I attribute this current divergence to the recent demand for commodities. Resource-based economies like Australia's traditionally outperform the stock markets of non-resource heavy economies during a commodity boom. This means the local sharemarket could continue to rally at a faster rate until commodities crash.

The time difference between Australia, Europe and the US means that the local market is open at different hours to the major overseas markets. As a result, many of our larger stocks which are listed on local and overseas exchanges 'gap open' rather severely. A 'gap' occurs when a stock opens the day at a price beyond the previous day's extreme; that is, above yesterday's high for an upward gap, or below yesterday's low for a downward gap.

BHP Billiton (BHP) and Rio Tinto (RIO) are prime candidates; they often move further up or down on a gap open than they do throughout the rest of the Australian trading day. This can make trading these stocks difficult, and discourages me from trying. Gaps on the open can happen to any stock, but some gaps are so common and so large that they make your best technical analysis-based trading useless – the distance you could normally trade on a short-term basis is swallowed up in opening gaps. Traders with a longer term perspective, who hold positions for weeks or months, would be less discouraged by gaps, as they are less concerned with short-term volatility generally.

A significant move higher on the Dow generally helps our local market rally. The Dow made a triple-digit move higher last night; looking at the local share charts it seems that the Australian market was already anticipating this upward move.

Being a break-out trader means that I prefer to buy as soon as the price of a stock exceeds recent or old highs. I learnt early on in my futures-trading days that a stock is never too high to buy or too low to sell. When a strong bull market is happening, you can forget about 'buy low and sell high' – that's a pipe dream. It's a case of getting on the bus and not worrying whether you get the front seat or the back seat. The longer you're in the trading game, the more you'll understand that the important thing is not your entry, but your management of the open position and ultimately your exit.

For this reason I rarely use a limit order. Instead I enter at market and, unless there is a big gap in price between the break-out level and the current bid or offer, I accept the market price. If there has been a significant jump away from the break-out level I might keep my finger on the trigger and wait until the volume returns to the market before I open a position. Pulling down the price depth window on my trading platform keeps me posted on the available volume.

Sometimes a stock breaks a key level at or near the open of the trading day and then pulls back. I've seen this happen many times with BSL and often wait for it to complete a pullback before I try to buy.

This morning, BSL gaps open and then rallies above its recent high of $8.36, which happened on 20 June. I decide to go long for another 2000 BSL and my order is filled at $8.39. It tops at $8.40 and then starts to fall again. Figuring that a close below the day's gap open price would be a negative, I cut the whole position at $8.30. I more or less break even on the cumulative position.

If a stock I'm trading does not behave the way I expect it to, it's usually a sign I should get out of the trade, even if I haven't made a loss on it – unless of course it runs into a much bigger profit much faster than expected. If I buy on a break-out near the start of the day and then the stock goes back down, a move below the day's low is usually my sign to exit. This is because a test of the upside has effectively failed and a test of the downside is now on the cards.

Newcrest Mining (NCM) is a stock that often has a very thin order book (limited liquidity), but I'm a sucker for big ranges, and NCM can move more than $1 during the course of a trading day. This stock also trends nicely, which offsets the relative illiquidity. It might typically trade a **spread** as wide as ten or fifteen cents, especially after a key support level or resistance level has been broken. This stock can really move, so I rarely wait for it to narrow the spread before I jump in.

I see NCM take a fall and then rebound just as fast. With the price of physical gold down US$4 overnight (physical or 'spot' gold is always quoted in US dollars), the obvious trade was on the short side, but the obvious is often a trap.

If NCM closes below $16.50, this will be a break of major support and confirmation of a topping pattern. The downside test takes it to $16.58 before it rallies hard. Because NCM is a thin stock, its price can be pushed around and there are always plenty of false break-outs. I get set for a long position at $16.77, a price which represents the first break of resistance since the $16.50 downside was tested and rejected. I watch the stock pull back and then buy some more when it goes above the pullback high of $16.93. My total long position in NCM now is 2000 share CFDs.

I go to lunch and come back to discover the stock's been all the way up to $17.09 and then fallen back below $17.00 again. It has done exactly the opposite of what I had anticipated earlier in the day, when I decided to open the first long position. It has made a quick move higher and just as quickly retraced those gains. I've missed the cue, so I work a stop at $16.89. I base my stop-loss level on a recent resistance level that I expect to turn into a new support level.

It is not until the end of the day that NCM reaches my predetermined stop level. I take the whole position out at the close. This is not always the best time to trade, because prices can be very volatile in the last few minutes. The Director says that, on average, 30% of the day's business is executed in the last ten minutes of trade. I ask him about other Aussie share CFDs that can be extra volatile into the close, and he mentions ARC energy (ARQ), Brickworks (BKW), CSL Limited (CSL), St George Bank (SGB), Perpetual Trustees Australia Ltd (PPT), Cochlear (COH), Macquarie Bank (MBL), Sims Group Ltd (SMS), Publishing and Broadcasting (PBL), Caltex (CTX), Rio Tinto (RIO), Woodside Petroleum (WPL) and Wesfarmers (WES).

If you are trading long-term, liquidity on the close is not as important, but because I tend to hold positions for the short-term, building a position over a few days or a week or two at most, the need to exit or enter on the close is high and therefore I need to take closing volatility into account. CTX is the only stock on The Director's list I usually trade.

One of my daily habits is to check the market action 'into the close'. If it seems likely that a stock's movement will finish strongly, taking out recent resistance levels, I am often encouraged to enter a trade before the market closes. I like this entry technique because a stock with this kind of price action will often gap open the following day. Today's end-of-day run-down leads me to take two long positions into the close.

My first long position is Excel Coal (EXL) for 1500 at $7.57. EXL gapped higher on the open this morning and then rallied throughout the day, breaking out above its resistance level at $7.57. This resistance dated back to 23 June and had been tested and rejected on the daily chart on each of the subsequent trading days. The more often a level is tested and rejected, the more significant it is when the price finally breaks through. EXL settles the day at $7.60, which means I'm three cents in the money.

The other trade I carry out near the close is in Jubilee Mines (JBM). I buy 2000 at $7.07. JBM makes a similar pattern to EXL, closing above its 23 June high for the first time. It finished the day at $7.12.

# Day 3

Thursday, 30 June
Total: $12,764

---

I didn't sleep well. Small dog woke up three times in the night, once to sit by his food bowl and cry. He's never done this before. I'm superstitious, so I take this as a bad omen.

Before the session starts I check my open positions and make sure stops are placed on everything. I place a stop on Excel Coal (EXL) based on an intra-day support from yesterday's chart. I also place stops for Jubilee Mines (JBM) and Aristocrat Leisure (ALL) based on previous intra-day support levels.

At the beginning of the session I am stopped out of two of the three positions I have open. The first one is ALL. Being stopped out too early and watching the trade go back into profit is more painful – much more painful – than getting stopped out on an ordinary losing trade. I moved my stop-loss level up, making it extra tight. If I had left it where it was originally, it would have kept me in the trade. I make a $10 loss. When I'm not making money generally, these kinds of events have more impact on me. When my account is riding high, they don't matter. I'd like to get to the point where, win or lose, the profit or loss from a trade never matters. Ashley J says opportunity cost cuts deeper than the normal loss – when a winning position is not taken, it causes more regret than a position which is closed out for a normal loss.

EXL goes as low as $7.39 and I get stopped out at $7.47. I'm getting chopped up – getting stopped out or 'hit' going long or short – because the market is rangebound. I was hoping that once I started writing the trading diary I would make money right off the bat, but that isn't happening. Just as markets trend, so can your profits or losses. I fear that I have started off in loss mode and that this might be a trend that has some course to run.

Maybe part of my problem is entering on daily close data, but working stops based on intra-day data. I do this as a way of circumventing my $350 rule. When I see a good trading opportunity based on a closing price, I tend to work a stop-loss based on an intra-day level. This is because a closing price entry is usually a long way from closing price stop-loss levels. Setting a stop-loss level in this way is essential for a longer term trading approach. In order to take such a trade over the short-term prudently and with discipline, I would have to take a much smaller position size, but this kills the fun, so I tend to work my normal size position but use a stop based on a 30-minute chart. This is clearly tempting fate: an entry based on an end-of-day signal often needs more room than one based on a 5-minute or 30-minute chart entry signal.

Every successful trader will tell you that the only way to trade any kind of market successfully is to have the right psychology. I used to read a lot of books about positive thinking, but they aren't helping me now. I decide to take a more drastic measure. Years ago I read about a technique called neuro-linguistic programming (NLP), a way to reprogram the brain. I decide it is worth a try, and I search the net for an NLP therapist. I find a woman who does both hypnotherapy and NLP.

I go to my first appointment hoping I can turn my new losing streak into a winner as quickly as possible. I expect to be on the therapy couch, listening as the therapist tells my subconscious that I am a happy trader, enjoying abundant wealth and success, but instead she's dragging up the past. Parents, ex-boyfriends, flatmates, anyone who has had an influence and contributed to my negative thinking. I cry, but she tells me this is normal. She ends up presenting me with a bunch of negative statements – damaging beliefs about myself – that affect the way I see things without me even knowing it. The plan is to start to reprogram at my next session, replacing the old negative statements with new, positive ones. She assures me it's not like traditional therapy, in which it takes years to work through your issues. The idea with NLP is to identify the negative selfbeliefs and then start changing these unconscious thought patterns in order to stop making the wrong choices.

# Day 4

Friday, 1 July
Total: $12,069

---

With the Dow down nearly triple digits this morning, I expect some of my stops to get hit. Spot gold was also down, so my small long position in Newcrest Mining (NCM) is likely to be stopped out on the open, given the stop-loss order I left in place yesterday. Gold stocks don't always follow the index lower, but I check on my trading platform. The US gold share index is down just under 1%, and NCM follows suit, falling around 15¢. The stock opens down on yesterday's close and continues lower. I work a tight stop and lose less than $200.

I see Centennial Coal (CEY) test the upside and meet resistance at the highs of the last two days. I take this as a negative, so I take a short position. I am wrong. The price rallies and I'm taken out on my stop-loss before the end of the day.

I also take a short in Computershare (CPU). I've been burnt by placing too tight a stop on this stock before, so I drop my position size to take a wide stop. I go long Patrick Corporation (PRK) after it breaks a basing range. I place a stop under the basing range.

All of the positions I've taken so far were made on the basis of easily observed support and resistance: I worry that perhaps these trades are too obvious. I keep thinking about a comment from The Director that the smart money does not think like the crowd.

They say you should be thankful when your first trades are losers, because this teaches you a greater respect for the markets from the beginning. If you have already started trading CFDs and your first trades were losers or you've had a losing streak, you should be able to relate to the experience I'm having now. If you have been trading for a long time, you know that losing streaks can last weeks or months and getting back into a winning phase might mean adjusting position size, working smaller stops, taking fewer trades or not trading at all for a while. One thing's for sure, getting back in the zone takes a mental/emotional shift.

---

### The story so far

Profit/Loss to date – $931 loss
Closed positions – 10; Open positions – 4
Winners – 3; Losers – 7; Win/loss ratio – 0.30
Biggest loss – $287; Biggest win – $203
Number of consecutive losing trades – 5

---

Not a great start. Five losers in a row is a tough beginning emotionally. Biggest losing trade is larger than the biggest winning trade, which isn't a good sign either. Win/loss ratio not great. My obvious problem is that I'm setting my stop-loss levels too tight. This is a common error made by new traders. It inevitably leads to the use of stops that are too wide; traders overcompensate, going too far in the opposite direction, and incurring bigger losses as a result. Also, I must make use of lunchtimes to grasp profit-taking opportunities and adjust stop-loss levels.

# What have I learnt?

- If I use closing price data to enter a trade it follows that I probably should use closing price data to plan my stop-loss levels. Instead, I have been using intra-day data. I need to consider my late-in-the-day entries in light of this and maybe reduce my position size, since it is resulting in me getting hit on too tight stop-loss levels.

- End-of-day volatility needs to be considered. Big swings in the last few minutes are the result of heavy volume as traders re-position themselves into the close. For short-term traders, the volatility some stocks show in the last ten minutes of trading is too great, so it might be a good idea to avoid trading them altogether. (The stocks The Director listed for me are good examples.)

- Watching as a position is stopped out and then seeing it go back into profit is very painful. I have to combat this feeling and be prepared to enter again.

# Do's and don'ts

- Do have the right psychology, because it is everything. If you are new to this game, I know you won't believe me, but the sooner you grasp this concept, the faster you'll become a consistently successful trader.

- Do be thankful for your losing trades, especially in the beginning. They are your most important trading lessons.

- Don't start trading until you have a plan, even if it is something as simple as entering on a particular pattern or indicator and exiting with a trailed stop-loss order. Trading without a plan is just gambling.

# Lingo and lessons

## Trouble pulling the trigger?

The opposite of impatience is not being able to pull the trigger: waiting too long to enter a trade. This happens to me when I'm in a losing spiral – I tend to stay out of good trades when I feel that I can't stand any more losses. My trading coach has a simple solution for not being able to pull the trigger, an approach that is especially well suited to CFD trading because the commission rates on CFDs are so low. He recommends taking small trades on which you will pay a maximum of $10 in commissions, and then simply buying and selling until pulling the trigger ceases to be an issue. This might mean holding a position only for a few minutes and then getting out. The idea is to get accustomed to the entry and exit procedures, diminishing the fears associated with the trading process.

## False break-out

A false break-out occurs when the price goes beyond a support or resistance level, confirming a break-out, but instead of following through, it retreats back inside the break-out point.

## Spread

The distance between the highest bid price and the lowest offer price is called the spread. The wider the spread, the higher the cost of trading. For example, assume that the last traded price on Aristocrat Leisure (ALL) is $12.50, with a current bid price of $12.40 and an offer price of $12.55. This is a 15¢ spread. If you were to go short at $12.40, you would be selling at 10¢ below the last traded price, and the stock's offer price would have to fall to $12.40 before you could buy back and break even on the trade. If we imagine instead that ALL is trading a narrower spread of $12.49–$12.50, anyone deciding to sell at market would be set at $12.49. That's a 9¢ improvement on the wider spread quoted in the first example, and the stock's offer price would only have to move down 1¢ before the trader would break-even. Always consider your break-even price before entering a trade. You will find a more detailed discussion of spread in my first book, *Contracts for Difference*.

## Targets for chart patterns

A 'target' is the price you expect a stock to achieve or fall to following confirmation of a pattern.

Once there has been a break-out from a pattern, the target – that is, the minimum distance you expect the price to travel from the break-out point – is determined by taking the vertical distance or height of the pattern and adding this distance to the break-out point for a bullish break or deducting it for a bearish break.

To determine the minimum target of a rectangle, first calculate the vertical distance between the base and the top of the rectangle, and then add this figure to the break-out point. For example, looking at figure 1.1, you will see that the value at the base of the rectangle is 10 and the value at the top the rectangle is 20. You would subtract 10 from 20 to find that the vertical height of the rectangle is 10. When you add this to the value of the break-out point, 20, you will arrive at a minimum target of 30.

**Figure 3. Determining targets for chart patterns**

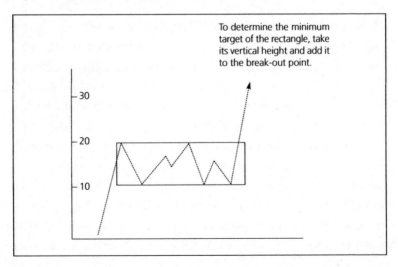

To determine the minimum target of the rectangle, take its vertical height and add it to the break-out point.

# Trading tip no. 1

## Stop-loss level based on the opening price

Old chart highs are significant. A strong close above an old chart high is a buy signal; however, if a stock breaks resistance intra-day, but can't go higher, and then starts to fall back, it's a sign of underlying weakness.

The chart below shows price movements for BSL throughout June 2005. I was already long 2000 BSL share CFDs when the market opened on 29 June. I bought another 2000 parcel near the open after it gapped. However, there was no follow-through, so I worked a stop-loss order for the total amount just under the gap open. The price moved down, fell below the gap open, and continued to fall. When there is a gap open to the upside and a rally, a good point to place the stop-loss is just under the opening price.

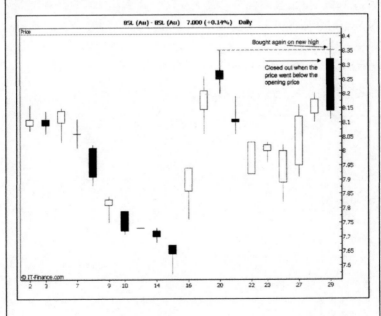

© IT-Finance

# Week 2

## Lunch is for wimps

## Day 5

Monday, 4 July
Total: $11,703

---

On Saturday night I'm at a party. A guy walks in who I dated a few years ago for about six months. I haven't seen him since we ended. He looks uncomfortable, but the only people he knows at the party are in the circle I'm standing in. He comes up to my group and he starts talking. 'You were right about gold,' he says. One of the last times I saw him I was just starting to get bullish on gold; recommending stocks like Normandy (no longer on the board because it was taken over) and Lihir Gold (LHG). He is an accountant, which is not much better than an economist when it comes to understanding how to trade. At the time he disagreed with me, giving lots of reasons why gold wouldn't go up. Back then it was trading under $300 an ounce. This was around the time I started dabbling in small gold shares.

I have been short Ventracor (VCR) for a few days, getting set at $1.36 on Thursday. David L says you can't call yourself a trader unless you are prepared to go short. 'Just because you are comfortable with the idea of going long and you have been profitable, it is not an excuse,' he says. 'If you don't equip yourself with the skills to trade on the short side you are letting some of the best market opportunities pass you by. Take a look at a chart of the local index. You can see it spends most of the time heading upwards, but when it falls, it does it swiftly. You could say that markets fall about twice as fast as they rise. Knowing this, it is obvious that you can make a profit more quickly in a falling market than a rising one. Sadly this does not relieve you of the responsibility of picking which way the market is going to move in the first place – but after all, that's half the fun.'

VCR has spent a long period of time trading a relatively small width range, suggesting that it could have a swift and potentially large move lower once the range is breached. Today the stock finally makes a bold sell-off. After it breaks support dating back to early June at $1.32, I add to the position from 30 June, doubling my initial stake of 4500 shares at $1.31.

When I'm looking for an exit point in trades like these I take the vertical distance of the sideways range and deduct it from the low of the range. In this case, the first congestion range gave a target at $1.30. The break of $1.32 is the confirmation of a double top with a target under the $1 mark. In a few minutes it has already fallen to $1.26, but it quickly establishes a spiky looking low. Despite this, I decide the winning trade doesn't need much attention and go upstairs to make lunch for a friend. I don't trail the stop or add a stop for the additional trade. We sit outside on the deck at my house, looking at the sea. Suddenly small dog vomits in front us and then starts eating the vomit. That has to be a bad omen.

After last week's Newcrest (NCM) trade caught me out at lunchtime, I should have known better than to walk away unprotected today. VCR can be whippy and, true to form, it had a massive rally. I went downstairs to discover I had already given back all the day's gains and my winning position had turned into a loss. When you add to a trade, the worst case scenario is that you end up taking a loss on the collective position.

Before the close I exit at $1.38, losing $427 (more than my per-trade limit of $350). I could have exited before lunch with a profit of over $600. Lunchtimes can see some rapid movement. This might prompt some traders to widen their stops; others might view lunchtimes as an opportunity to make a smart profit on short-term trades. Why is the period between midday and 2.00pm often so volatile when I presume most of the professional money is out to lunch? I ask The Director.

'It's herd mentality,' he says. 'Many large institutions may step out of the market at lunchtime which means that they pull any orders they are working. What's left is the herd – retail clients chasing each other. This means the order book gets thin and becomes prone to gapping and poor trading conditions.'

That sort of explains it, but sometimes when I'm long a stock like NCM I've seen the high of the day occur during extra-thin lunchtime trade. I think, to play it safe, the more volatile stocks should be watched over the midday break.

I have been taught a couple of good lessons today. The first is that I should remember the importance of price action over lunchtimes – it's worth placing limit orders on profitable trades for at least part of your position. The second is that I should keep the big picture in mind. When the outlook is as bullish as it is now, short positions must be treated with extra attention. The VCR experience reminded me that in a strong bull market volatile stocks can make enormous short-term gains. A quick scan of the S&P/ASX 200 shows some of the real dogs of the index, such as Multiplex (MXG), have been joining the rally. Even if it proves to be more dead cat action, bull markets exert upward pressure even on the best looking downtrends.

'Trading is all about learning lessons as you go,' says David L. 'I have spoken to many traders and the one thing they all have in common is that they are still learning. There is no course, book or mentor that can give you the whole picture. At the end of the day, we all have to get into the market and learn a good portion from experience. The market is a dynamic beast, so your understanding of it also needs to be dynamic. The rule of rules is that we need to keep our capital preserved continuously so that we can always be in the market to learn new things.'

# Day 5

Tuesday, 5 July
Total: $11,772

---

I start the day by compiling the Top Ten Sell List for InvestorWeb. Every month I write a technical analysis-based Top Sell and Top Buy list and once a week I do a market overview of the S&P/ASX 200, the Dow Jones, the Aussie dollar, gold and crude for the site. This is a great exercise for staying in touch with the wider market. However, there is one downside to my work for InvestorWeb: forming definite opinions can compromise my trading.

'I like to think I'm very good at taking advantage of opportunities,' says The Director. 'I have always been a medium-term holder of equities – whether I go long or short. I am not a fundamental trader or a technical trader; I'm just driven by the numbers – not by my opinions. That's how I was taught to trade. And it wasn't how I was taught by an individual or a book, it's how I taught myself.'

The idea of trading without an opinion isn't easy for me to accept. I am paid by InvestorWeb to have an opinion, get a kick out of having that opinion proved right, and spend much of my time with friends and acquaintances swapping opinions about things. Having an opinion is human nature.

'Super dynamic trader' is the name David L gives to the best traders. 'They have an opinion about anything they are trading, but it can change and become the polar opposite in the blink of an eye,' David L says. 'You need to have an opinion sometimes, or why else would you have any positions? The key is not to fall in love with your opinion.'

When it comes to trading, having an opinion can be your downfall. How can you stay open-minded when you trade? One way is always to imagine other possibilities. For InvestorWeb, I generally write a commentary with two scenarios – the bullish and bearish alternatives – although it's usually obvious where my real opinion lies. This means I am never proven to be completely wrong, but it also forces me to consider both sides of the story. The longer I've been an analyst for InvestorWeb, the more particular I've become about presenting both sides of the story. It saves a bunch of told-you-so's on the InvestorWeb chat room if I make a wrong call. Before the correction of late March 2005, I warned IWL subscribers to tighten stops and take some profit as there was a possibility that there was a correction coming. I added a caveat – that they should buy again if the market showed more strength. I called it an insurance policy. This created quite a furore (a furore for me is about two threads in the chat room forum). I hadn't met with such virulent opposition before; investors clearly had much at stake on the long side. As a result, I suspected there was a good chance of a decent correction, and that was exactly what happened between late March and early May 2005.

With the US market closed overnight for the 4 July public holiday, I expect today to be quiet, and it is. I don't take a single trade, but I do see good consolidation in a few of my positions, namely BlueScope Steel (BSL) and Hardman Resources (HDR).

The hypnotherapist calls. A relative has died and she cancels my appointment until next week. My losses have been growing since our first meeting. A week can be a long time when you are a short-term trader in a losing streak.

Unconventional ways to stay in the zone are commonplace in the trading world. Since I've been in the business, I've interviewed quite a few very successful large-scale traders. Some of the most seemingly conservative, old school male traders, the types who dreamed of owning a Porsche in the 80s, are now doing yoga on the beach at dawn.

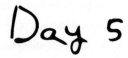

# Day 5

Wednesday, 6 July
Total: $11,293

---

The Dow resumed trading last night with a healthy gain. There's a common phenomenon on the local market when the US stock market has a big up move: after a significant rally on the Dow, local shares often open higher and then slowly give back the gains throughout the day. Dealing with this requires the ultimate contrarian mind and is a big test of the 'no opinions' philosophy.

Contrarianism is a school of thought that says conventional beliefs and views of the market do not make money. By taking the opposite view of the majority opinion, the smart trader isn't caught in the madness of crowd behaviour. When the Dow has a healthy rally overnight, the natural urge is to buy the local index or stocks, but often prices fall and the best strategy is to sell.

I've traded BSL often enough to notice a fairly regular pattern of opening gains followed by a quick sell-off. I would need to see BSL go above its old resistance level of $8.36 before I'd be prepared to add to the position. I'm glad I don't add to the position before the stock reaches this level, because it travels to $8.28, a break of a recent range, but then sells off to close down for the day.

In my opinion, closing prices are more important than opening prices. The Director's revelation that 30% of trading activity happens on the close backs this up. Intra-day activity on light volume can take prices to extremes that are quickly forsaken when traders square up towards the end of the day. Closing prices are more indicative of market sentiment than opening and intra-day prices because the close offers the last chance to alter a position until the market reopens the next morning. For this reason I do a quick re-analysis of the markets in the last half-hour of trading. I scan the charts to see how my current positions look and to check for opportunities to open new positions on the basis of closing activity.

I check the price for Aristocrat Leisure (ALL). It's currently showing a 19¢ spread. Even if I liked the chart action, the spread indicates that there is a lot of potential volatility in this stock, especially coming into the close. I have seen this ALL move 20¢ between its closing price at 4 pm and the ASX auction settlement price which appears around five to ten minutes later.

I decide to take a trade on the Materials Index. It has the advantage of being commission free and I can use stop orders to enter a position. A 'stop entry order' allows me to enter a trend as soon as an order level is breached.

The Director tells me that the most successful sector traders take long-term positions in index CFDs, usually going long, since the market has been bullish for so long. Other sector CFDs include Consumer Discretionary, Consumer Staple, Energy, Financial, Health, Industrial, Information Technology, Materials, Telecoms and Utilities. I take a small short position of five lots or index CFDs with a wide stop. I also go short Coles Myer (CML), because it breaks below a tight consolidation range it has been trading since 30 June.

# Day 8

Thursday, 7 July
Total: $10,829

---

The Dow is down around 100 points, and with so many long positions coming into today, I expect some carnage. Amcor (AMC), BlueScope Steel (BSL), Patrick Corp (PRK) and Consolidated Minerals (CSM) all get stopped out. I only have one short position of any size and that's Coles Myer (CML). I have a small short in Computershare (CPU), but it initially rises. The Materials Index is also buoyant in the first few hours of trade.

I wait until near the close to take more short positions, in case some of the obvious breaks of support rebound late in the day. I end up going short David Jones (DJS) for 5000, short BSL for 5000 and short another 1000 CPU. I am still long Hardman Resources (HDR). Despite the rise in the oil price overnight, HDR is down 7¢, but it is still above my entry of $2.20. This implies that energy stocks will still be hurt even if crude keeps rising and putting a dampener on the general stock market.

This brings me to something every trader should be aware of – the relationship between a company's share price and the price of the commodities it produces. Crude oil prices can rally, but this doesn't necessarily mean that all resource stocks will rise. Today, for instance, when crude made new all-time highs overnight, Arc Energy (ARQ) and Hardman were down, while Caltex (CTX) and Santos (STO) were up. Gold is also interesting. For the last week, Newcrest has been trading a narrow range just below its 30 June highs, but spot gold has had a sharp sell-off since then. 'The rule here is that the market is always right,' says Ashley J. 'Basing trading decisions on expectations rather than the reality of price action is probably the main reason a trader loses money.' The longer term trend implies that energy shares and crude oil prices are correlated, and so are gold stocks and the spot gold price, but on a short-term basis, it is not always the case.

A journo mate calls me today with the news that the Australian dollar gold price is currently at the top of a trading range and looks as though it is ready to break to the upside. I am a long-term gold bull, one of those people who think this precious metal could end up trading in the four digit range before the gold bull market is over. Every gold bull has been waiting for gold to rally against currencies other than the US dollar. That's meant to herald the start of the true bull market for gold: a time when Aussie gold stocks, especially the junior gold companies, should start to step up.

# Day 9

Friday, 8 July
Total: $10,825

---

I am at a bar when the news comes of the London terrorist attacks. I don't think anyone in the markets likes to admit it, but even though these kinds of events are shocking at first, your next consideration is the effect on your open positions. After the Madrid attacks I wrote an article about unexpected events and their effect on the financial markets. I concluded that although markets gyrate somewhat, trends established before such events usually continue. Events like the September 11 terrorist attack on New York and the Madrid bombings were not turning point events.

I arrive home from the bar and check the FTSE. The chart wasn't looking toppy before the event; there was no established downtrend or overextended rally. It's down 3%. It's tempting to trade something for the local effect, but less than an hour later, the UK index is rallying hard, which proves my theory that the new London terrorist attack will not be a turning point in the market.

I add up the underlying value of my short positions versus my longs. I have just over double the value of shorts to longs. I feel safer being on the short side, but I know the market could go either way tomorrow. One thing's for sure – it won't do what everyone expects – which is a big sell-off.

I ask The Director about these kinds of big, unpredictable events. He was on the desk in London during the September 11 attacks on the World Trade Center, and was head trader in Sydney when the Madrid bombings happened. 'The first question traders should ask themselves is the moral one – should they participate in any big swings following such an event?' he says. 'If they decide that they have no qualms about trading in these circumstances, Aussie traders will usually react to an event in, say, Europe or London by taking a position on the Aussie 200. If you're accustomed to watching overnight action on the local index, you'll know this market is exceptionally thin, so the first response to bad news is generally a gap down. However, these events are characterised by volatility, so traders who are short following an event like the London bombing should be aware that the market's short-term direction will be led by UK activity. A sudden reversal and rally on UK stocks, like the one that happened last night not long after the bombing news, is generally the trigger to buy back after an event. Looking at the larger overseas markets at a time like that is your best guide for direction.' As I end the conversation, The Director calls me a carpetbagger.

---

### The story so far

----------------------------------------

Profit/Loss to date – $2175 loss

### This week

Closed positions – 7; Open positions – 12
Winners – 0; Losers – 7; Win/loss ratio – 0
Biggest loss – $445; Biggest win – $0
Number of consecutive losing trades – 7

---

Tough week, not a single winning trade and a run of twelve losses in a row that started last week. The VCR trade left a scar. Big losers, especially when they were previously winners, tend to take an emotional toll. Am also feeling unnerved by the London bombing. A big negative event, one that I can't control, has broader implications. The future of the world just became a little less rosy.

## What have I learnt?

- Learning lessons as you go is what trading is all about. You can't learn it all from a book. Making mistakes is part of the journey. As soon as you start trading, you are on the learning curve. I have to remind myself of this even when I'm in a losing streak.

- A problem with technical analysis is that a majority of traders are looking at the same charts and waiting for the same patterns to be confirmed. That's why a technical signal will often turn into a false break-out. When I am entering on a break-out I try to check the price depth information on my trading platform first, to make sure there is plenty of underlying strength behind the move. Strength is indicated by a good number of bids, if I'm buying, or offers, if I'm selling.

- I had a second hard lesson in lunchtime price action. I can't afford to let a position out of sight during the period between noon and 2.00pm, even if I think a trade looks safe.

## Do's and don'ts

- Do reduce your position size when you are trading a wider stop or when you are in a losing streak. Reducing position size is an important money management strategy.

- Do check the underlying performance of relevant commodities when you are trading a resource company. For example, when you are trading CTX, you'll need to watch crude oil. The relationship is not necessarily straightforward. Check the US or UK sector index, this will also give insight into the general underlying sentiment.

- If you want to call yourself a 'trader', you must embrace the concept of going short. You might not find many opportunities to do so in a strong bull market, but eventually they will appear. When this happens, going short may be the only consistent way to make money on the market.

# Lingo and lessons

## Determining stop-loss levels

When selling, I always base my exit stop-loss levels on old chart support. Occasionally I'll use an old resistance level, but I find in the short-term that the last resistance level is often breached and then the price keeps going higher. When a stock breaks a level but then returns to the trend, this is called a 'false break-out'. Some stocks behave in this way more frequently than others. Check the price history of individual stocks to see if this is a regular event on their charts; if a stock has a tendency to false break-out, make sure you give your stop extra room.

David L has a couple more stop-loss level strategies. He uses the low price from a set number of days previous or the 'parabolic stop and reverse' or SAR. The parabolic SAR is not something you can easily calculate yourself, but your charting software can usually do it for you. I've never used SAR myself, so for a good explanation of the SAR, go to the website www.investopedia.com.

## Lunchtimes

Some stocks, particularly volatile ones, can move a long way between 12.00pm and 2pm, so this is a good time to place a limit order to take a profit on at least part of a profitable open position. It is also a good time to be cautious about acting on entry signals. Lunchtime break-outs can be funny business – extra volatility, sharp reversals or spikes and low volume counter-trend activity. It's worth monitoring individual stocks' behaviour over the midday break period. Some will be more likely to follow through on the break in the afternoon session than others.

## Sector trade example

The best sectors to trade are the most popular ones – materials and finance – because they have the best spreads and are therefore likely to be less gappy. It is important to realise the sectors market opens fifteen minutes after the 10am open. This is to accommodate the alphabetical opening of the exchange. Until all the stocks which make up a sector index are open for the day, an accurate sector price cannot be supplied. As a result, you will often see a major gap on a sector when the market opens for the day and some fast trending in the first fifteen minutes of trade. For that reason, sectors are better suited to long- or medium-term trading strategies.

The spreads quoted on the different sectors vary depending on the liquidity of their underlying constituent shares. My CFD provider, one of the few providers of sector trades, require a margin of 1% of the trade size multiplied by the sector value. For example, let's say the Materials Index is trading at 7322. You buy 5 lots at 7322. The margin requirement is calculated as follows:

Margin required    =   Sector value x trade size x 1%  
                   =   7322 x 5 x 1%  
                   =   $366.10

# Trading tip no. 2
## When unexpected events occur, stick to the trend

September 11, the Bali bombings, the Madrid bombings, the London bombings – my study of historical chart action shows that prices may fluctuate immediately following an unexpected event, but they soon return to the existing trend. Don't take a trade after an unexpected event or catastrophe unless the pre-existing price action supports the direction of the news. The UK100 index chart below shows that the index was in an uptrend when the London bombings occurred. There was an immediate sell-off, followed by a resumption of the upward trend. The long tail on the final candlestick on the chart shows the great distance between the low of the day and the closing price: a clear rejection of the downside as the uptrend resumes.

The trend is up before the London terrorist attacks. The immediate reaction is increased volatility, but the uptrend does not end. Note the long tail on the candlestick, which is a bullish sign.

UK100 – UK100  5733 (-0.05%)  Daily

The trend is up before the London terrorist attacks. The immediate reaction is increased volatility, but the uptrend does not end. Note the long tail on the candlestick which is a bullish sign

© IT-Finance.com

© IT-Finance

# Week 3

## Into the abyss

## Day 10

Monday, 11 July
Total: $9304

---

The fallout from the London bombing is negligible. There is some extra volatility on the UK market, but US and local commentators are attributing any other movement to the action of crude prices and domestic data. It proves my theory that after some short-term gyrations, long-term trends are not affected by a sigma event. In fact, when I was researching my story about unexpected events, I looked at the period leading up to the 1987 crash. There was no significant event, economic data or commentary by fundamental analysts that suggested the world stock markets should have chosen that day to crash.

The local stock market index closed on Friday above its correction low of a month ago. When a market tests an old low by trading below it intra-day, but then closes above that low and inside the range, it can be a good reversal signal. Today proved that theory when the price continued higher. The buy signal came when the index went above Friday's range high and there was more bullish indication when it closed at the top of a relatively large range – it's never too high to buy. The next big thing I am watching for on the index is a close above the old highs. If that happens, it will be the third test of the old high of 4321. The more often a level is tested and rejected, the bigger and faster the move that follows when it finally does break.

I move my stop orders closer, having seen a big move higher on the Dow on Friday night. As a result, my shorts are nearly all closed out today. I'll narrow a stop-loss level if I think the big picture has changed overnight. Making this decision isn't easy, because the big picture can change from bearish to bullish, but you might still have a dog in the pack that won't follow through to the upside if there is a general market rally.

My general feeling is very bullish: I think even the dogs are likely to have some large rallies today, even if these gains are not sustainable in the long-term. A couple of months ago I started building a portfolio of short positions I hoped to hold for the long-term. At that time there were plenty of stocks showing medium- to long-term weakness, many of them issuing profit warnings and results that were lower than expected. I got the idea of the long-term short portfolio from a fund manager friend. An advantage of this strategy is that you are paid interest, even if your positions merely languish rather than fall seriously. However, most of those positions were taken out when the market started to reverse in early May. Such is the strength of the bull, even property stocks are starting to look like they want to rally, but as this bull market eventually loses steam, I believe the rallying activity will become narrower and more focused. Some sectors will top before others and this is when the best shorting opportunities will arise.

Thinking about shorting in a bull market makes me wonder about being a contrarian. Is it a good thing? I ask The Director if he sees most winners in the contrarian camp. 'The smartest traders I know are contrarians,' says The Director. 'They might have a long-term view, but they would never allow it to interfere with their everyday responses to the market. You have to think like the average trader, but then form your own opinion. This comes naturally to contrarians, because they are constantly thinking laterally instead of in a linear fashion. So to be a smart trader, you must embrace the obvious, take a common sense approach and then stare at the numbers, considering them from many different angles. If nothing comes to you, then don't trade, even if this means you go for weeks without trading at all. It doesn't cost you anything not to trade.'

My account drops beneath five figures today for the first time. I feel bad. In ten days of trading I've lost over $3000, including commissions I've paid. My account balance is in a nosedive.

I ask The Director about the typical mistakes of losing traders. 'The worst traders always blame the broker – it's always the broker's fault – or they blame the trading platform or the market – "The market did it to me!" '

The Director thinks my problem is that I feel pressure to trade successfully for the sake of the book I'm writing. 'You're starting from a really bad position,' he says. 'If you feel you have to make money, you're probably doomed. If that feeling is constantly on your mind, you'll lose money.'

The Director reminds me of a story in the book *Reminiscences of a Stock Operator* in which a group of traders decide to have a competition to be the first to make enough money from trading to buy a fur coat. 'It was a story to show that this trader Livermore was God,' The Director says. 'He could make money from anything, but when he was put under pressure to achieve a particular objective, he blew himself up. It happens to everyone I know. Even the best traders blow up when they set themselves a particular goal about how much they have to make. If you put yourself under pressure to make money your tendency will be to lose a lot of money. It's happened to every trader I know. For instance, if you're an institutional trader and you make $1 million, the head of the dealing desk will say, 'You're a good trader – now you must make $5 million. Three months later you'll be down $2 million and then you'll burn out and disappear for a few months. Some traders can make a recovery, some of them can't.'

My trading coach calls to confirm our meeting for tomorrow. I tell him I'm feeling emotional. I can't seem to shake the cycle of losses. He says that just as a pilot still has to land the plane even if he's feeling sad, traders need to leave their emotions out of the trading room. I'm not so sure I can.

# Day 11

Tuesday, 12 July
Total: $8797

---

With eleven straight losing days of trading since I started writing this book, I'm staring into the abyss.

I have a 7.00am meeting with my trading coach. His aim is to turn me into a supertrader. We start off having breakfast at a cafe near his hotel. I tell him it has been really hard, that I've lost money pretty much nonstop since I last saw him at the supertrader weekend program he ran in June. My account has been on the decline ever since I started writing the book. I usually take a trade history for him to analyse, but today I don't even bother to give him the details. It's too depressing. I tell him I feel like going home to bed and crying.

The first thing he says is that this is normal. Every trader goes through a period of serious loss in the early stages which brings up larger emotional issues to be dealt with. That's when many traders give up.

We discuss my concerns about the book I'm writing. I'm worried that male traders won't be able to relate to wanting to bawl when things get tough. He says he's had sessions with male traders who cried at losses, but adds that men tend to handle emotional difficulties by getting angry, or might not express their pain at all. He tells me another of his clients has blown up recently, a trader who was trading a much bigger account than I am. Hearing about someone else's failure makes me feel better.

We go back to his hotel room and he starts the coaching session. He doesn't use the kind of clichéd motivation techniques that some other coaches do–there's no ra-ra hype. Instead he takes me through two guided meditations. Neither of them has me bouncing off the walls, but I leave feeling like it's possible to make money again. Do I have the character, though, to keep me out of the abyss?

An hour later I'm at my trading desk. I make some trades that start to move in my favour quite quickly. After taking only one trade yesterday, I take seven trades today – all long positions, except for one. By the end of the day I exit one position, the volatile Caltex (CTX), because it didn't take off and I don't want to risk an overnight gap. The rest close at healthy levels.

# Day 12

Wednesday, 13 July
Total: $9236

---

I only take one new position today, and that's to increase a long position in Hardman Resources (HDR). I exit my short position in Excel Coal (EXL) for a profit. Taking a profit on a short when the general market is rallying gives me a real kick. In a strong bull market, shorts are hard to take in the first place and even harder to exit without getting burnt, so I congratulate myself. A general rule when dealing with shorts is to be scrupulous with your trailing stop-loss. To prepare myself psychologically for leaving a short quickly, I usually work out possible downside targets or exit points early on – identifying levels in the market where a fast reversal might occur. These levels are based on old resistance that might turn into support, or old support levels where the price has bounced before, or Fibonacci levels. When these levels come into play, I watch like a hawk to see whether the market is happy there or if buyers start stepping in.

I have my second appointment with my hypnotherapist. It's time to reprogram my thought patterns, replacing old, discouraging thoughts with new, constructive ones. I've done my homework and have a list of positive outcomes she's asked me to bring for this session. She taps my head a few times and counts me down to what she describes as a state of deep relaxation. I don't feel deeply relaxed. (I am definitely conscious enough not to take my clothes off on command.) The hypnosis process allows one part of my subconscious to heal another. The therapist tells me that my conscious mind remains fully present while she does the therapy. I worry that nothing is happening, but when she tells me to wake up, I start laughing for no reason (or maybe just because I feel silly).

At the end of the day I realise I haven't actually lost money from my account in the last two days but I haven't gained much either. Is this the breakthrough? If my account balance could be charted like a share price, I would be encouraged: narrow, uninteresting price action after steep falls can be the basing pattern before a recovery. Then again, it could also be a consolidation pattern before more losses.

# Day 13

Thursday, 14 July
Total: $9767

---

I forget to remove a stop-loss order. It was protection on a short position in the Materials Index which I closed out today, so now I have accidentally taken an extra five-lot long position. Since the position is not looking bad, I decide to keep it rather than jump out immediately. The Director says when it comes to errors, traders always remember the error trades that made them money, but not the ones that lost them money. A good rule is always to exit a trade taken in error. Unfortunately, I don't and later it bites me in the proverbial. I take a loss of more than $500 on the combined position of 10 lots.

Trading errors is a bad habit of mine. In the old days, when I was a futures broker, if I made an error on a client account and it turned into a loss it came off my salary. I used to try to work the error to avoid having to wear the loss myself, especially if it was discovered when the position was already against me. Since I've been trading CFDs the only time I've made money on an error was when I was already in the middle of a great winning run on my account. Maybe if you accidentally take a trade when you're in the zone, it could be your subconscious putting you onto a winner and you should stick with it. Possibly, then, this is the best rule: if you collect an accidental position when you're in a losing streak, kick it out of bed straightaway, but if you take a trade in error when you're in the zone, keep it and work it. (Sounds like I'm playing with fire.)

# Day 14

Friday, 15 July
Total: $8824

---

Before the market opens I telephone the US to interview a guy called Jim Puplava. He is to be the subject of an article I'm writing for *Your Trading Edge* magazine. Puplava runs the website www.financialsense.com. As much as I'd like to be cool like The Director, unmoved by opinions and experts, this guy gets me really excited. He has stacks of commentary on his site from some of the coolest contrarian commentators, including Marc Faber of the GloomBoomDoom website; Jim Rogers, the co-founder of Quantum fund; Bob Prechter, an Elliott wave expert; and Richard Russell, a Dow theory expert and author of the longest running financial newsletter. Puplava doesn't charge a cent for access to his site. He is a fund manager, which is how he makes his money. He has his own regular column on the site.

Puplava is making some big calls – he tells me that gold is going to $2500–$3000 an ounce, and oil will reach $100 a barrel. High oil prices are another pet topic of mine. Before the recent US-led war on Iraq I went on Bloomberg and said oil was going to go up no matter what the outcome of the war, because a strong long-term uptrend was already in place.

I also love Puplava's gold comments – I've been a diehard gold bug since 2001, when I started recommending gold stocks on InvestorWeb. I'm hanging off his every word. He thinks spot gold bottomed in May this year and is now about to enter the next cycle of the uptrend.

When you have a contrarian opinion and you meet another contrarian, it's wonderful. It's like being a nomad in the desert and then one day coming across another nomad: you realise how much you've missed hanging out with a tribe. Zealous contrarians can lose friends (try telling your home-buying friends it was the wrong time to buy two years ago). Worse still, if you are a contrarian too early, you'll inevitably lose money; many times you won't even make any money when the time is right. The trick is finding the balance between getting set early enough to beat the pack, but not so early that you lose money while you wait for the pack to cotton on.

Puplava makes an important point about buying gold stocks when he compares this sector's performance to the tech boom of the 1990s. If you bought IBM in 1990, when it was the big name tech stock, you would have paid $20. At the same time in 1990, Dell was trading at 4¢. By the end of 1999, IBM was selling at $140 (seven times its 1990 value), but Dell's stock was worth $56 (1400 times its 1990 value). If you buy Newcrest Mining and hold throughout a 10-, 15- or 18-year bull market, you might make seven or eight times your money. (NCM has already reached levels over five times its 1998 price high of $2.95). However, picking the next Dell equivalent could return ten or twenty times your initial investment. A few of these cheaper stocks can be traded on the Aussie market with CFDs. Croesus (CRS) comes to mind because it's cheap, but I've had more success trading Oxiana (OXR) in the past. Other small gold stocks include Ballarat Goldfields (BGF), Gallery Gold (GGN) and Oceana Gold (OGD).

---

### The story so far

Profit/Loss to date – $4176 loss

### This week

Closed positions – 18; Open positions – 11
Winners – 5; Losers – 13; Win/loss ratio – 0.38
Biggest loss – $359; Biggest win – $426
Number of consecutive losing trades – 8

---

I have winning trades on the board, even if the biggest was a measly $426 profit. This week has been better than last week, when I didn't make a single profitable trade. Still, nothing to write home about. Realised that taking a profit on a short position is a great feeling – best not to get greedy on these trades when the market is so bullish. I feel like I've turned an emotional corner, but the results are not showing in my account. Something's got to give.

## What have I learnt?

- The pressure to make money for the sake of this book might be taking its toll. I think this pressure hinders anyone who is trying to trade with a specific goal in mind, such as paying for a holiday or buying a house.

- Working or trying to profit from an accidental or error trade on my account is probably not a good idea. If I am already in a losing streak when it happens, I think it's definitely a bad idea. If I am in a winning streak, though, it's probably worth keeping it but only with a tight stop-loss order in place as insurance.

- When I pass from a losing phase into a winning streak, the emotional shift comes first. When I feel like a loser, my trades all seem to be losers, too.

## Do's and don'ts

- Do keep focused on the price action and not on the imaginary profits. This is the lesson of the fur coat story.

- Don't beat yourself up about losses. They are normal, and every trader has them. If you chastise yourself when you lose on a trade, you may find that you start trying to avoid losses by hesitating to work stop-loss orders.

- Don't think you can predict the effect of an unexpected event on the market. Stand aside and wait for clear indications of movement that is consistent with the prevailing trend.

# Lingo and lessons

## Fibonacci levels

In the 1100s, an Italian mathematician, Fibonacci, came up with a number system formed by adding two numbers in a sequence to produce a third, until infinity, as demonstrated below:

$$1 \; 1 \; 2 \; 3 \; 5 \; 8 \; 13 \; 21 \; [\infty]$$

The division of any two numbers in the Fibonacci sequence (after the first three numbers) always creates a number approaching either 1.618 or 0.618. This numerical relationship is known as the golden mean. Other Fibonacci derived levels are 0.382, 0.236, 1.618 and 2.618. They are used in trading to identify potential turning points in price movement. For more information on Fibonacci, try *Fibonacci Applications and Strategies for Traders* by Robert Fischer (John Wiley & Sons, 1993) or *Trading with the Gods* by local Aussie trader and author Alan Oliver (Alan Oliver, 2004).

## Remove stop-loss orders after you exit a trade

Some CFD traders only execute stop-loss orders if you have an open position. If you accidentally leave a stop-loss order on a share CFD after you have closed a position with one of these providers, it won't be executed if the price gets to the stop-loss level. If you are trading sectors or indices, the situation is different. Stop-loss orders can be used to enter a position, which is great for break-out trading, but you must never forget that a stop-loss order left in the market can potentially be executed to give you a position. If you forget to remove it you will be liable for the position. You cannot expect your CFD provider to forgive your mistakes.

## Losing money is normal

No matter how many times you are told that losing money when you trade is par for the course, it still feels uncomfortable. When you start trading, be prepared to lose. If you are serious about trading, and plan on doing it for a living, you will face big losses and be forced to learn from them. This is normal, but that doesn't make the lessons any less painful. Decide now if you have the character to deal with losses. If you have any doubts, get some therapy or forget about trading altogether.

## Trading tip no. 3

### Entry signal on an intra-day breach

When a market ventures outside a basing or congestion range on an intra-day basis, testing the previous lows but closing well inside the range, it's a bullish sign. You could take an initial buy by entering just before the close. This can be tricky if the price is close to the range low and moves significantly with the auction. Alternatively, you could buy on the following day when the stock breaks the previous day's highs.

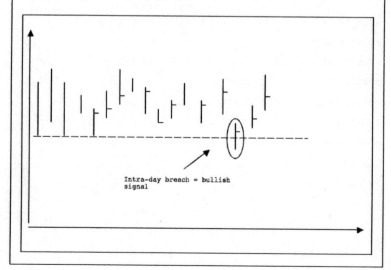

Intra-day breach = bullish
signal

# Week 4

## Wealth god smiles

## Day 15

Monday, 18 July
Total: $9455

---

David L has taught a lot of new traders, and says that something they all have in common in their first attempts to educate themselves about trading is a tendency to focus on the more complex and mathematical charting techniques. 'You should understand that the amount of money you spend on your charting package has no correlation to your returns,' he says. 'Remember, Charles Dow, the father of technical analysis in the Western world, worked with a pencil and ruler. Many of the ideas which have been developed from his original scribblings are based on simple movements of price. Traders should never forget this. Although there will always be newer and more complex ways of approaching the same problem, many of the methods that have survived since the early 1900s are as effective today as they were then.'

It took me years to understand the importance of keeping it simple. It wasn't until I worked with one particular futures broker, an ex-Chicago floor trader, that I changed my thinking on this topic. He forced me to go back to price action. Even though I had passed my technical analysis exam years earlier, I had to hit the books again and relearn the basics. It was a turning point in my approach, because it allowed me to establish a basic, profitable strategy from which I was able to evolve my own trading style. The next step, though, is to manage your emotions, and that's where I'm at now.

I start intensive hypnotherapy today – two sessions a week. We haven't touched on the issue of money or career or anything that is related to my trading. Instead we are talking about parental baggage of which there is apparently quite a bit. 'If I fix the bigger emotional issues will it stop me losing money in my trading?' I ask the hypnotherapist. She reminds me that the big issue we are working on is rejection and that suffering a loss in trading is just another form of rejection. A losing trade is the market telling us to get lost. It's not that different from the rejection that our parents inadvertently subject us to. It appears that your average middle-class upbringing in small town Queensland can engender some insidious beliefs. I hope my mother doesn't read this.

# Day 16

Tuesday, 19 July
Total: $9294

---

Something's working. I exit a profitable trade today. I bought 1500 BlueScope Steel (BSL) share CFDs at $8.35 on 12 July, and closed it today at $8.76 for a profit of $615. I usually trade 2000 BSL at a time, but this time, with my confidence wrecked and my losses mounting I had decided to pare back the position size.

I was also stopped out of three losing trades today for a prudent total loss of just $278.

Lately I've been thinking about the wisdom of taking short positions. When the big picture is bullish, as it is right now – something which has recently been re-affirmed by a close above the highs on the index – going short is a risky business. Adding to short positions is probably even more stupid. The problem, though, is that on days when everything is turning down I'm not sure how else I can make money. I suspect it might be better to stay out altogether while the market pulls back, and be content to look for early safe buying opportunities I can take up once the correction is over. Still, short trades are extra tempting, because markets tend to move lower more quickly than they move higher.

It is very common for a market that makes new highs or breaks a key level to fall back either to the original break-out point or below it. The price retreat forces out the lightweight bulls who can't handle losses and sucks in some trigger-happy bears, often me included, but these reversals are frequently short-lived, and the resumption of gains can be brisk, leaving behind the stopped out weak buyers and creating a classic squeeze on short traders.

In an overheated market it's better to buy at the break of highs and run with it, but if the break of highs isn't followed by overheated buying, it is best to wait for a pullback and buy on the second break of the highs. I find the more rapidly a market reaches a high, the more likely it is to pull back or correct when it gets there. A slow and concentrated move upward to meet new highs is more likely to have the substance to follow through.

Since the S&P/ASX 200 reached a new all-time high on 20 June, only a couple of days after I started writing this book, it has been trading sideways beneath this level. The sell-offs have been limited, but I have taken too many short positions in anticipation of more downside. However, the upside has also been limited: in fact a perfect series of three tops and two bottoms have formed. This is good news, because the greater the number of times a top is tested and rejected, the further the price will go if and when it does break through. Long positions taken on the back of this action are likely to yield the best trading opportunity that I've had since I started trading for the book.

# Day 17

Wednesday, 20 July
Total: $9922

I am walking along the street this morning, about to start the trading day, when I find a dollar coin. I've had some luck finding money on the street before. About once a year I find a wad – sometimes $200 to $300. I once picked up $200 in two neat $100 bills. I was walking with a friend, so I gave her half, and the next day I got a parking ticket for $90. Still, finding money, no matter how little, is always a good sign. In my superstitious world, it means the wealth god is smiling on me. They say it's bad luck not to pick up money you find on the road: it's like telling the wealth god you don't need it. Worse still if you drop money and don't bother to pick it up. I once dropped a bunch of coins running for a bus when I lived in London. My life was a fiscal nightmare for a long time after that.

Even though the Dow is up over 70 points, it doesn't mean the local index will gain, and it definitely doesn't mean my particular long positions will move higher. The worst days are when the Dow is up, the local index is up and my portfolio of longs goes down. That happens more often than you might imagine.

This is partly explained by the composition of the local market index. The stocks given greatest weighting are BHP Billiton and the top four banks, which gives the index a finance sector skew. 'To have an opinion on the general market index, you need to have a view on BHP and the big four banks, because they make up over 30% of the index weighting,' says David L. When the big cap stocks are in favour, the mid-cap stocks (the stocks I usually trade) are often less popular.

My star trade of the day is Excel Coal (EXL). I made money on the short side last week: it was the first winning trade of any size I'd had since I started. I've had some good wins in the past with EXL. I think I have an affinity with this stock. I call stocks like this 'harmonic' because they trade in a way I find a little more predictable than others. When I exited that short position, I waited a day for it to prove itself on the upside and then I bought into the close of the second day. It wasn't the best entry, because I could have bought earlier and lower, but I made sure I gave it plenty of room, leaving a stop at $7.02, which was 2¢ below the low of the day I entered the trade. Yesterday the price made lows of $7.03, just one hairy cent above my stop level, before rallying. It had a mediocre close, so I held off buying more. When it opens today, it quickly goes above yesterday's highs and gives my favourite ever buy signal – it completes a small range double bottom. These patterns are good for two reasons. The first is that they give you the ability to get in and work a tight stop-loss. If the double bottom is very narrow, you can leave a stop-loss just under the lowest leg of the pattern, which is usually, but not always, the first leg. (The trading tip given at the end of week 10 gives an example of a chart showing a double bottom pattern.) The second reason is that the double bottom pattern is often the start of a sustained rally: a double bottom means that the downside has been tested and rejected twice. The upside is usually much bigger than the textbook minimum target for a charting pattern.

My first entry is at $7.19 for 1500; the next is at $7.25 for another 1500. EXL closes the day at $7.46. Just before the end of the session, I buy another 1500 for $7.48.

Some stocks are a safer buy on the close than others. My two favourites to enter at close are BlueScope Steel (BSL) and EXL. Ironically, the best time to buy into the close is when a stock has already had a big run higher that day and especially if a lot of that buying was done late in the session. EXL definitely meets that criterion today; and over the past few months it has frequently had runs of successive big up-range days, many of these with a gap up on the open. The great thing about being a chart follower is that when a pattern occurs, I can get a good idea of what a stock has done in similar circumstances in the past. I look back at the EXL chart and notice that these big range days have a habit of coming in threes. If that's right, tomorrow should be another day for big moves to the upside.

# Day 18

Thursday, 21 July
Total: $12,916

---

Excel Coal (EXL) gaps up on the open, making yesterday's trade on the close seem like a moment of sublime insight. The position moves from a profit of $714 at yesterday's close on the three-entry position to a fantastic $2053 on the open. The benefit of adding to positions is exponential. If I'd been content to stick with my initial long position of 1500 share CFDs at $7.19, I would be up a measly $915 by comparison. As the price eases, I get a bit spooked, so I close 1500 out at $7.77, but it doesn't like the downside and rebounds after reaching a low of $7.70. I buy more when it goes above the morning's high of $7.85, getting set at $7.88. EXL finishes the day at $8.15; my combined position, plus the profit on the closed trade, is $3628.

If all I ever did was trade small range double bottom patterns like the one that EXL confirmed on Monday and then pyramid, I would probably avoid a lot of losing trades and make much more money. The last time I saw my trading coach, he told me that when I'm in a losing streak, I should stick to my sure-fire trades. I didn't give it much thought until I saw EXL make the set-up for the perfect reversal and basing pattern. The next time I'm going through a losing streak, I should step aside, and only take trades when I see this pattern – and only when I am looking at charts for stocks which have proven this pattern works.

I talk to author Eva D before lunch. She's putting together a book of testimonials from CFD traders. 'The one thing that all of the top traders I spoke to told me was that they don't worry about losing money anymore, because they know they can make it back again,' she tells me. The more often you enter the spiral of loss and come through it, the greater the confidence you acquire in your own ability to persevere into long-term success.

My winning streak extends to more than just EXL. I have good profits in Coles Myer (CML), a position I added to two days ago, and I take half the position out today as it pulls back. I am up on Jubilee Mines (JBM), and when it takes out the old highs (something this stock seems to do regularly), I buy some more.

Newcrest Mining (NCM) has been a baddie this week. Puplava's comments about gold made me keen to buy NCM and too quick to add to the position. I was stopped out of two attempts to add, leaving me with my original long position of 1000, which had a different, lower stop-loss level.

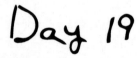

# Day 19

Friday, 22 July
Total: $13,794

---

Excel Coal (EXL) gaps on the open and races higher again. My position of 4500 looks too good to be true, which is usually a sure sign I should be taking a profit. I see it trade above $8.40 very quickly, a move of over 20¢ above yesterday's close, and I immediately move my stops in tight. I place a stop-loss order for 3000 at $8.29, because the only place the price paused on a swift move to $8.48 was at $8.30. I watch it as it pulls back and hovers around $8.40. I contemplate exiting, but soon enough it's down again, gapping from $8.40 to $8.35, then a few ticks to $8.30. Once the 3000 are out at my $8.29 stop-loss, I walk away to get a drink. I come back and the stock is trading in the $7.80 range. Luckily I had a stop for the remaining 1500 at $7.97. I'd forgotten about it, because I hadn't expected the price to fall to that level. This good fortune – a positive mistake on my account – is perhaps a result of being in the zone.

It comes all the way back to $7.30, just above the original double bottom highs of $7.24, the price at which I started buying. I check the chart history for similar big moves higher followed by large corrections. These kinds of events are usually followed by a few more days of volatility and are not that easy to trade. I decide not to push my luck and don't re-enter. I book a total profit on the scaled-in position of $3763. If I'd stuck to my original position and hadn't added to it, my total profit would have been just $1155.

I end the week with a third attempt to add to my Newcrest (NCM) position. Unlike the other two, it doesn't get stopped out. At the close, the original position is up 16¢ and my second addition is 2¢ in the money. I might finally have found the right entry level. I also buy Oxiana (OXR) today at 93¢. I've always liked this stock and it's a cheap and a less volatile opportunity to get gold exposure.

Pick up any self development book and you will invariably come across the story of the guy who failed and continued to fail until one day he got lucky and then became phenomenally successfully. They say the difference between a successful person and one who lives a life of mediocrity or failure is the ability to get over loss and rejection and start again. Becoming a successful trader involves frequent trips down that street. In a normal career, you face loss relatively rarely, but as a trader, loss is a regular and unavoidable fact of life. How you deal with loss will decide whether you survive and thrive or give up in despair.

When I first entered my losing phase I knew in theory that trading is cyclical, and that I would enter a new winning phase sooner or later.

In reality, though, I was fearful that I would not be open to the good times to come – the losses had been so consistent that losing money was starting to feel normal. After my visit with the trading coach last week and a couple of sessions of hypnotherapy, I felt that things were turning around, even though my account hadn't made any progress. Until you start trading, you can't realise the emotional importance of the experience. If you are trading and regularly losing money, and blaming this on your chosen system, it might be time to explore the losses, looking for an underlying emotional element that you may be reluctant to face. If it's significant, I guarantee you won't succeed until you've taken steps to deal with it.

---

## The story so far

------------------------------------------

Profit/Loss to date – $794 profit

### This week

Closed positions – 16; Open positions – 14
Winners – 8; Losers – 8; Win/loss ratio – 0.50
Biggest loss – $526; Biggest win – $1532
Number of consecutive losing trades – 3

---

This time last week my account was down over $4000. My account balance is now in the black for the first time since I started writing this book. Win/loss ratio not much improved, but there is a big difference in the size of my winning trades. I booked four trades with profits over $500 and two trades with profits over $1000.

## What have I learnt?

- I pat myself on the back for persistence. NCM was a good example. I kept trying to add, but getting stopped out. I stuck with it. My third attempt has been the most profitable so far. I don't know how it will end up, but I like the fact I am not running scared when I get it wrong. Most traders give up on a stock too quickly when they get early trades wrong.

- The winning cycle always returns, but the trick is to survive in the meantime. I lost a lot of confidence waiting for my losing streak to turn around, but with some sensible advice and mental 'reprogramming', I was able to prepare myself emotionally to make money again.

## Do's and don'ts

- Do keep abreast of the general index. This will tell you if you are trading with or against broader market sentiment.

- Increase your appetite for risk when you are already trading well. If a position is already in profit, adding to it is more likely to pay off. The middle and later stages of a trend are where the largest and fastest gains can be made.

# Lingo and lessons

## Scaling-in creates big winners

If I have only one winning trade in ten, but that one trade reaps $3000 and the rest are losses of $300 each, I break even. A run of ten losing trades is rare, but when you scale into or pyramid a winning position the gains can go exponential. Your win/loss ratio is unimportant if you are pyramiding winning positions. Combine pyramiding with the leverage factor only available from CFDs and you truly have the holy grail of trading CFDs profitably. Like any other investment product, CFDs can be risky if you don't work a stop-loss. The risk you face in trading CFDs is directly related to your level of discipline as a trader.

## My strategy for gaps

Whichever direction the stock gaps is the way you should trade; that is, if it gaps down, you should sell, and if it gaps up, you should buy.

However, this depends on the size of the gap. If a gap down isn't too big, you can buy if the price goes above the range of the first half-hour. Similarly, you can sell on a small gap up if the price falls below the range of the first half-hour. Holding into the close on a winning trade will maximise results.

Work a stop-loss just beyond the extreme high or low of the day, depending on the direction of the trade. If you set it any closer, you could be stopped out and then find that the trade goes back in your direction.

# Trading tip no. 4

## Entry signal on the close

When a market rallies into the close it can be a sign of more upside on the following day, and often an opening gap, too. I regularly see strong rallying occur in series over three-day periods, which implies it might be related to the ASX T+3 settlement rules. I took advantage of this phenomenon with EXL this week, a stock which has behaved this way several times in the past. The EXL chart below shows that there were three gaps in a row. The final gap was followed by a huge sell-off, but my tight trailing stop still made it a profitable additional position. Not all stocks behave this way. Check historical price data to see if a particular stock is suitable for buying on the close.

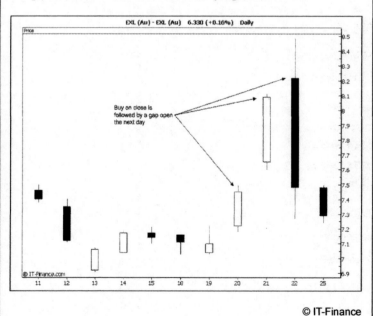

© IT-Finance

# Week 5

## Avoiding Waterworld

## Day 20

Monday, 25 July
Total: $16,016

---

In the morning I'm on my regular run to Bondi Beach with small dog when I pass two separate groups of middle-aged men. I overhear both groups talking about the sharemarket. When any investment sector becomes a hot topic with the general public, it usually means it's in the final stages of a bull cycle. When average everyday people – those I like to call the Johnny-come-lately's – are getting excited and talking about it, this is the time when the biggest gains can be made. This section of the investing community can turn a bull market into a bubble.

My winning streak continues today. My affection for Newcrest (NCM) is finally reciprocated. The stock trades briefly below its opening price and then moves upward, eventually breaking the recent range high at $16.32. I watch it continue to $16.42 but then it pulls back. I see a smaller base forming before I buy another 1000 share CFDs at 16.34, taking my total position to 3000. NCM closes the session at $16.69: I'm up over $1900 in just one day. This stock is whippy. If I was trading Excel Coal (EXL), for instance, I would have added another parcel on the close, but I know from past experience that NCM can make lightning moves higher and close on the highs, but then open $1 lower in the following session. I don't think this is likely tomorrow, but I want to play it safe. I've made so much profit recently that I'm in danger of doing something reckless.

I started with $13,000 in my account just over a month ago. At the close of trading today my trading platform blotter tells me that my account balance stands at over $16,000. Last week it was down at around $8000. These gains have been largely due to two positions: EXL and, as of today, NCM. Hit rate – your number of winning trades versus the number of losing trades – isn't that important if you can keep your losses small and add to your winners. If you only have a couple of really big winners, it can still make a huge difference to your profits.

I tell The Director I've had a great run with my trading and ask him about staying in balance. 'How can you avoid the ego trade?' he repeats. 'You can't prevent the urge.' He relays the wisdom of a floor trader he once knew, who told him that when he started in the business he was dollar wise and cent foolish. The only reason he was still in the business was that he became cent wise and dollar foolish. It is the small and medium-sized trades that keep a trader going; not every trade can be a big hitter. He learnt not to take the foolish big trades and risk everything.

Sticking fastidiously to a well-thought-out trading plan is always The Director's approach, but he also recommends that I try another strategy he uses to avoid the ego trade. He tells me to withdraw some money from my trading account to lower my balance and remove the temptation of overtrading or taking a big trade that I couldn't normally afford. 'It goes back to the idea of taking $1000 out of your account every week,' he reminds me. He suggests asking my broker to pay me with a cheque rather than a direct deposit. 'Cheques take five days to clear, so there's less opportunity to change your mind.' I like the idea of seeing my wins in physical form rather than just having them show up in my account the next day. I decide to withdraw the money at the end of the week, just like a pay cheque.

At 7.30pm I call my trading coach. We have arranged a regular 15-minute catch up on Monday nights. He says it's no surprise I've done well since my last session, because he believes in me. I tell him about my NCM trade. 'Was it right to keep adding when I was stopped out?' I ask. He believes that holding a small stake is a good idea when you first enter a trade, even after you have realised a profit, because it keeps you focused. I realise if I'd stopped myself out of the whole position I would have walked away and probably not traded NCM for a while. Holding on to the small position of 1000 share CFDs, despite having been stopped out twice on scaled-in positions, kept me vigilant. The more closely you watch a stock, especially from the beginning of a trend development, the better you will know it and the more likely it is that you will ultimately be able to trade it profitably.

# Day 21

Tuesday, 26 July
Total: $15,672

I'd like to use today's diary entry to discuss the greatest feature of CFD trading – leverage. When I was in my losing streak, my account balance was nearly halved. This limited my ability to take positions, because I simply didn't have enough money in my account. At some moments I had less than $1000 left after covering margin requirements and my losing open positions. As a position moves into profit, the amount gained is instantly added to my bottom line, increasing the capital available to trade with. In this way, leverage can boost your returns exponentially; a benefit a share trading account can never deliver. To increase the balance of a traditional share trading account, you have to realise your profit by selling shares. With CFD trading, the profits of an open position are immediately added to your trading account and can be used to fund further profitable trades.

'I would always say to clients, even those who are quite experienced, that they shouldn't use all the leverage available to them, not initially,' says The Director. 'The best way to be disciplined with margin is by scaling in. For instance, if you had $120,000 in your account, you could take a $20, 000 position in BHP Billiton (BHP). That would mean making a margin deposit of $600. It's easier to manage than risking a significant amount of your capital trying to buy 10,000 share CFDs on BHP at the outset. So instead of twenty to one leverage, use two to one. If you get it right – whether this becomes apparent in two minutes, two hours, or two days – scale in. Then, once the position is onside, start to use the leverage. It's a psychological thing. You need a position you can emotionally manage.'

With the Excel (EXL) and Newcrest (NCM) trades I was scaling in as per The Director's recommendation. Once my account started to rack up some small wins, I didn't worry about the leverage. My account benefited from large winning positions and the balance grew very rapidly, adding capital to my account which I could use for further trades.

'It's great to think you have the ability to run a big line of stock. I'm a fan of the glass-is-half-full attitude to life, but when it comes to trading I believe the glass is half-empty,' he adds. 'You need to be slightly pessimistic. Trading is about survival. You need to think initially about breaking even on every trade, and only then consider gearing. If you never gear yourself up too much, you'll never be in a position to get cleaned out. What I'm suggesting is that you put your stops in at various levels. If you are a medium-term trader, you don't have to get out in one clip. If you're going to sit in front of a screen all day, you'll be tempted to set stops mentally. You need to develop the discipline to stop yourself out. Leverage is your friend and your foe.'

I've been running graduated stop-loss orders with EXL and I've also applied the same strategy to NCM. Two previous added positions in NCM have been stopped out, but the original entry remains intact.

When the chips were down, I had no breathing space. I had to keep enough in my account to cover my margin. At the moment about one-third of my account balance is free to use. I'm prepared to do riskier things when I feel like I'm in the zone.

# Day 22

Wednesday, 27 July
Total: $15,928, US$72

I take a look at the spot gold chart. I try to forget Jim Puplava's declaration that the correction for gold is over, but it's too late, his opinion is firmly planted in my brain. Time to buy. In the last week spot gold has rebounded above its May lows again, so I decide to buy 50 ounces.

Although I am partially motivated by Puplava's comments, it's really the chart that makes me want to go long. Gold often finishes a large correction with a double test of the lows, which often appears insignificant in terms of time and price. It's a cheap trade if I work a stop-loss just under the correction low. With my CFD provider, stop-loss orders on products like sectors and commodities are not worked on the last traded price but on the offer price for a sell stop and the bid price for a buy stop. Therefore, you need to add some extra room on the level you see on the chart. The correction low is $418, but I set my sell stop-loss order at $416.

I like the idea of having one amazing life-changing trade in my trading career. They say in everyone's lifetime there will only be one tech boom or similar event, and resources booms only happen every thirty years. If you don't catch a boom this time around, you've probably blown one of the best trading opportunities of your life. If this really is the bottom of the gold correction, this could be a position I keep for months. I fancy the idea of taking a gold position and holding it until the gold market reaches its ultimate top, maybe years into the future. I read an article by Mike Swanson on the website www.kitco.com, posted a few months ago, giving reasons why gold stocks are now going up.

**Reason 1 – Spot gold is rallying against all currencies.** In the early stages of a gold bull market the spot price of gold and the US dollar have an inverse relationship. A rise in the gold price is traditionally accompanied by a fall in the value of the US dollar. For Australian investors this means a rise in the price of spot gold is accompanied by a fall in the US dollar relative to the Australian dollar, offsetting gains.

It's a widespread belief that when this inverse relationship between the spot gold price and the US dollar breaks down, gold should start to rally in earnest. I've heard this phase of the gold bull market called the 'remonetarisation' of gold – a time when gold rises in value relative to all currencies.

**Reason 2 – Gold stocks are outperforming the spot gold price.** The beginning of every gold rally in this uptrend to date has started with gold stocks leading the spot gold price; and since the May low of this year, gold stocks have, in fact, been leading the spot gold price.

While I'm at the Kitco website I read a story about uranium. A couple of months ago I was asked by a resources journalist writing for the business section at *The Australian* to give some market commentary. Afterwards I asked him what his favourites in the sector were. He liked uranium. It makes sense that alternative energy comes to the fore when oil gets expensive, but being a technical trader, I don't have any idea which companies in the index have uranium interests. I'll look into it.

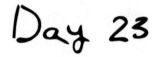

# Day 23

Thursday, 28 July
Total: $13,862, US$206

---

When I've had a big win in a stock I find it takes amazing discipline not to re-enter immediately. Despite my large win on Excel (EXL), yesterday I took a long position on this stock and even added to it. The result is a loss of more than $300 today.

I am clearly still susceptible to the ego trade. I have a businesswoman friend and she calls the ego trade by another name – Waterworld. She borrowed the name from the Kevin Costner film. At the height of Costner's career in the first half of the 1990s, he produced, directed and starred in a monumentally expensive movie flop. The film's tag line was 'Beyond the horizon lies the secret to a new beginning'. Beginning of the end, more like it. When you trade for a living, the ego trade – your own personal Waterworld – is always just around the corner. Anyone can make money from trading, but most people can only survive a limited number of personal Waterworld experiences.

Jesse Livermore, described as the world's greatest trader, infamously and spectacularly profited from the 1929 crash, but spent his trading career recovering from a series of mammoth wipe-outs. More recently, Victor Niederhoffer, a very successful fund manager achieving a compound return on his fund of 32% per annum every year between 1982 and 1996, went spectacularly broke in the 1997 Asian currency crisis. Niederhoffer is back in business now and has written a number of highly respected books on trading and life. Has Niederhoffer learnt the lessons of the past? Does he have the right amount of respect for the markets, enough humility not to go broke again?

It's all very well telling myself to be humble, and not be reckless, so that I won't end up in another Waterworld, but what are some practical steps I can take to avoid making a big mistake? As I ponder this question, the first thing I realise is that after a big win, I'm not usually aware that I actually start looking for Waterworld-style trades. If I'm still flying high following a recent success, I fail to recognise my subconscious agenda, which is to do something dumb. This means awareness is the first step in avoiding Waterworld. Having realised this, next I decide to go over my losing trades from recent times and look for patterns. I'm surprised to find there have been very few trades that resulted in losses greater than my usual $350 limit. They seem to happen only when a market gaps away from me or when I'm slack with a stop-loss order. I find that the losses have one key characteristic – most of them are the product of short trades. I also note that there have been very few winning short trades in my trade history while I've been writing this book.

# Day 24

Friday, 29 July
Total: $14,538, US$299

To help prevent the ego trade, I decide to act on The Director's suggestion that I try periodically 'paying' myself a nominal wage, taking the money out of my trading account. It's the end of the week, so I request a withdrawal of $1000. This should leave me about $1000 up on my original stake of $13,000. I ask for a cheque, which means I will get it hot in my hand – the withdrawal won't be just another meaningless figure on my bank statement.

In the past I've set goals to make a certain amount of money from my trading within a certain period, but it has never seemed to work. I ask The Director about setting profit targets. 'You need to have a target – a realistic target – and you need to have a plan,' he advises. 'A simple thing for a trader to do is to say, "I have $30,000 in my account, and my target is to make $1000 a week." You actually have to go to the ATM, draw out $1000 and put it right in front of you. Then you know: that's how much you need to make every week. If you count it out every week, forget about transaction costs, forget about brokerage – you want to make $1000 a week. Put it on the desk in front of you. It doesn't look like much – it's ten $100 bills. Visualise yourself doing it.'

Affirmations combined with visualisation are meant to help you achieve your goals. For the last week I've started the trading day by writing a page of affirmations. I try to come up with unique ways of saying 'I'm a successful, disciplined trader', 'I make stacks of money' and so on. Even though they seem to be working, I am petrified one of my flatmates might find these daily lines which look like I'm an idiot. Today I'm painting a piece of furniture outside my trading room. I get some scrap paper out of the bin to place under it. The paper is covered in my affirmation from a few days ago: something along the lines of 'I'm a money magnet, large profits flow into my trading account regularly.' I move the piece of furniture inside, and when I come back to pick up the mess, the pages of affirmations have blown away.

It's lunchtime and I'm surfing (trying to) with a freelancing friend of mine. 'Don't you love it when the ocean goes really flat? It means there's going to be some big mother waves coming,' he says. I immediately think about the markets. That same eerie quiet precedes a big move on a stock or index. You see it when a stock trades a narrow range over a few days or weeks and then suddenly explodes when the price breaks the range. Getting on board as soon as it breaks is probably one of the best trading opportunities around. It's also a cheap trade, because you can work a stop-loss just beyond the other side of the narrow range.

---

### The story so far

- - - - - - - - - - - - - - - - - - - - - - - - - - - - - - - - - - -

Profit/Loss to date – $1538 profit

### This week

Closed positions – 10; Open positions – 23
Winners – 5; Losers – 5; Win/loss ratio – 0.50
Biggest loss – $221; Biggest win – $1276
Number of consecutive losing trades – 4

---

I looked into the abyss; I think I found my character.

## What have I learnt?

- Adding to a position into the close works better with some stocks than others. This is a reminder that every stock has its own character and this character can change.

- Leverage is what makes CFD trading exciting. It is best used to add to existing profitable positions to achieve exponential gains – not to commit yourself up to the hilt on a single position.

- Placing stop-loss orders at various levels on pyramided positions allows me to remain in the market – and more committed to the price action than I would be if I were out of the market altogether. It allows me to increase my position time in the market, too, which helps me to take a longer term outlook than I usually would. That's a good thing, when you consider that holding in a bull market for the long-term is how the best profits are made.

- When I have a big win, I don't seem able to leave the market alone. After a momentous move, a stock is likely to enter a period of directionless sideways or choppy price action. This is the time to step back and wait. I find it very difficult to do this.

# Do's and don'ts

- Do step aside after big moves in the market. Let the market tell you what to do.

- Do take money out of your account when you have made profits. This helps prevent the ego trade and makes the online trading process more tangible.

- Don't do what most traders do, watching the big moves and trying to catch those. Be alert to boring price action; it can provide the best entry points.

# Lingo and lessons

## Withdraw funds regularly

I find money does not mean much unless you have it in your hand. I was presenting at a trading conference held at Star City Casino in Sydney earlier in the year. As I walked to my presentation, I passed a bank of automatic teller machines. I thought to myself, 'Would I be happy to risk money on trading every day if I had to physically take cash out of the ATM every time I wanted to trade?' The answer was no. Taking money out of your account makes the online trading process seem more real. It's also a good way to stop the ego trade. A smaller amount in your account equates to a reduced sense of success and less chance of doing something reckless. Placing the withdrawn funds in front of my computer screen in the form of a cheque also reminds me of the aim of the job at hand.

## Leverage – friend not foe

CFDs give you amazing leverage that the stock market can't provide, but leverage has a bad name. Everyone has heard the stories about traders who have lost fortunes trading leveraged instruments without a stop-loss, but there's no need to be frightened of these products: a stop-loss order limits the risk, and a guaranteed stop-loss order makes them literally risk free. Guaranteed stop-loss orders are another feature of CFD trading that neither the futures market nor the stock market offers. As their name suggests, guaranteed stop-loss orders guarantee you an exit at the price nominated even if there is a large gap or a crash in price. Using leverage with stop-loss orders is the smartest way I know to make money from trading.

# Remember to breathe

When you have just taken a big profit in a stock, it is wise to take a pause before buying that stock again. This is important in fighting the trading addiction. My first instincts are always to jump back in; however, I know from experience that I rarely turn a big winner into another big winner in the next trade. In fact the odds are much higher that I will trade a loser after a big winner.

# Trading tip no. 5

## Low volatility entry signal

One of my favourite buy signals after a correction is boring price action. When the sea goes calm, it's time to get ready to catch the next big wave. Boring price action means narrow ranges, little direction and sometimes intra-day price break-outs that do not follow through on the close. While most traders are drawn to volatility, the smart ones are stalking the dullards. Trading these kinds of moves also allows you to work relatively small stop-loss levels, because you can place your stop-loss order at the other side of the narrow range.

© IT-Finance

# Week 6

## Addicted to trading

# Day 25

Monday, 1 August
Total: $14,817, US$407

---

I'm meant to call my trading coach at 7.30 pm and I try to time it around a TV show on cable TV called *Elimidate*. I like this show because it reminds me of the lengths we go to avoid rejection. The show is a competition: either four guys try to win a girl or four girls try to win a guy, via a series of group dates, until only one contestant is left. I'm always particularly amazed at the lengths the women will go to when they are trying to win the man. My flatmate calls it a 'slut-off' and a 'bitchfest' because the girls invariably take astounding measures to advertise their sexual availability while at the same time insulting each other (or obligingly kissing each other if the guy suggests it). The thing that is most surprising, though, is that the man they are fighting for is nearly always an idiot. I suspect if you asked the girls what their motivation was, they wouldn't claim that the man in question was likely to be their soul mate, but rather that they didn't want to be rejected. Very infrequently, a smart girl will vote herself off because she realises the guy is a loser or that it's just not worth the fight.

Trading works the same way. Exiting a position at a loss feels just like failing or giving up; like being rejected by the market. Allowing yourself to get hit on a stop-loss order is a bit like deliberately voting yourself off *Elimidate* – you are choosing rejection. I am sometimes tempted to stay in a losing trade in order to put off dealing with those feelings of rejection. In the past I have sometimes moved stop-loss orders wider, in effect compromising myself to avoid taking a loss, only to take an even bigger loss later on. That's the kind of thing I do when I get into Waterworld territory. That's the kind of thing I should be making sure I avoid doing now.

I'm fifteen minutes late for my trading coach because Elimidate is now showing half an hour later than it used to. I don't bother to give him this excuse because it's flimsy and it won't do much for his impression of me as a disciplined supertrader. I tell him that after its dramatic reversal into profit, my account has been consolidating, but I'm still afraid of the ego trade. He reminds me not to be tempted to overtrade, to look for high probability/low risk trades and to stay focused. I don't find staying focused that easy. An ex-boyfriend once told me I had the concentration span of a mite.

# Day 26

Tuesday, 2 August
Total: $16,533, US$410

---

I ask The Director about stop-loss orders, which are, in my experience, the cornerstone of good trading. 'Some clients never use them,' he tells me. 'They use liquidation as a stop-loss. They basically open a position and it's all or nothing and they will run the position until they are closed out.' What percentage of Australian traders use stop-loss orders? 'In excess of 80%,' he says. 'It's high.'

'Our order book for stops is probably bigger in Australia than anywhere else in the world. Australian traders use all order types to reduce risk.'

# Day 27

Wednesday, 3 August
Total: $16,313, US$633

So far, going short has been one of my most consistent ways of losing money. If I know the big picture is hellishly bullish, I must control my urge to jump on short-term and mostly unprofitable short positions by staying focused on the big picture. Part of my problem might be that I rarely check the chart of the local index. A quick look at the S&P/ASX 200 is a good way to keep in touch with the market in general. Individual stocks can trade contrary to the index, but if the index is giving a strong buy signal, there is little point in expecting a significant move to the downside in any of my stocks. This was highlighted today when I compiled the Top Ten Sell list for InvestorWeb. The number of dog stocks in the ASX 200 making impressive basing patterns and wild upside gains is a sure sign that there are very few sellers out there. Even the property sector, the only sector that was consistently rubbish a couple of months ago, is going back up. This doesn't make sense to me – if the housing market has topped and the only question is whether it will have a soft or hard landing, what possible upside potential can stocks like FKP Property Group (FKP) and Australand Property Group (ALZ) have? But this time I won't let my opinion override the reality of the market. Property stocks are going up and therefore should not be shorted. However, I've seen some scary-looking downward gaps on these charts in the past, so going long is a risky business in this sector.

I exit my Newcrest (NCM) position after building the position I originally opened on 18 July. I make a total of $3176 profit from four different entries. The last time I added to the position was yesterday. I decide to sell for a couple of reasons. First, the spot gold chart looks like it might pause for a few days or even go lower. Second, as the day develops, the early session highs of NCM are not beaten.

I have a feeling I should exit a position I have in Hardman Resources (HDR). I buy 3000 share CFDs at $2.31 and then again at $2.47 for another 3000. The price reaches a new high of $2.56 in the uptrend today. I deliberate all afternoon but decide to leave the entire position open. It closes at $2.49.

# Day 28

Thursday, 4 August
Total: $15,023, US$684

---

I hate that lingering feeling you have after you've taken a profit on a big winner – the feeling that you got out of it too early and left money on the table. Yesterday I was tempted to leave 1000 lots of Newcrest (NCM) in the market but I didn't. Gold rallied another $5 overnight and I know that my NCM position would have gone higher today … if I still had it. Luckily I didn't cut my Oxiana (OXR) position or my spot gold. I scaled in and that combined position on OXR is now up over $1000. The spot gold position is nicely in profit since I entered at US$423.90 on 27 July and, after an explosive move overnight, the total profit on the trade is over US$600. Because I hope to keep this position long-term, I don't want to add to it yet. A correction back to the level I originally bought at, or perhaps even lower, is still on the cards, so until we see the extent of the reversal from current levels, I'm happy to keep my position to a meagre 50 ounces.

I take one trade today that is close to an ego trade. After I scaled into Hardman (HDR) and saw it close at a healthy $570 profit yesterday, crude prices were hit overnight and HDR gaps down 23¢ on the open. I am stopped out at $2.26, losing $780. It reminds me that being complacent in a winning trade is a sure way to become a loser. Anyone can enter a profitable trade. The smart thing is getting out with at least some of that profit. This is where a keen trailing stop-loss strategy comes into play.

I can't keep myself away from NCM today. I buy again when the price gaps higher on the open. It trades up 10¢ and then sells off slowly for the rest of the day. I'm stopped out for a loss of just over $200. Even though I was aware of the pitfalls of trying to get back into a big winner, I did it anyway. It seems that some trading behaviour is just plain addictive.

Once you've tasted success from trading, it's hard to walk away forever, even if you suffer huge losses. The attraction of fast money, effortless enterprise and gains achieved even while you sleep makes trading addictive. Trading for a living from home is probably one of the most popular dreams of baby boomers and generation Xers alike. The flipside is the challenge, the pain and the humility. It takes great strength of character to live through the losses. There is no other activity that has such an immediate and irrefutable impact on your selfworth and selfbelief. If you run a business, you can blame your employees, customers, the economy or the weather when things go wrong, but when you trade, try as you might, you can't ultimately blame the markets or your trading system or your broker.

# Day 29

Friday, 5 August
Total: $15,709, US$656

Today I'm writing about uranium stocks for my weekly InvestorWeb article. I check out Paladin Resources (PDN), the only uranium specialist in the top 200 list of Australian companies. PDN has uranium interests here and in South Africa. The chart suggests the horse has bolted, but I remind myself of a favourite saying, 'a bull market will go further than anyone expects'. PDN has had a good recovery since reversing yesterday at $1.41, but with straight-line gains from $1.30 up to $1.84 during July, it looks top-heavy, so it might need to revisit the $1.41 level again. I'll add it to my watch list.

A good example of the effect of the ASX auction after the 4pm close occurs today. I am long Aristocrat Leisure (ALL) from $12.45. At 4 o'clock, ALL closes at $12.60, but the auction price gives it an official close at $12.39. My ALL position goes from a nice profit to a loss. I've often seen this happen with this stock.

ALL is one of five positions I take today. Only one of those ends in the back when the market closes and that's Excel Coal (EXL). This is the third time I have added to the original long 3000 position I acquired on 27 July (1500 at $7.40 and another 1500 added at $7.49). Today's entry is for another 1500 at $7.59. I take this trade as EXL completes a basing range from the $7.23 lows to highs of $7.58 and then back to lows of $7.33. This is close enough to a double bottom pattern and a good reason to add, even though there isn't much space between my first entry, my second entry and today's entry. I'm prepared to be more aggressive with this stock because I've traded it well in the past; it's one of the stocks I think I have an affinity with. It closes the day at $7.70 – so far I'm right. The total position closes up $930.

---

### The story so far

------------------------------------

Profit/Loss to date – $2709 profit

### This week

Closed positions – 18; Open positions – 17
Winners – 7; Losers – 11; Win/loss ratio – 0.39
Biggest loss – $656; Biggest win – $1083
Number of consecutive losing trades – 6

---

I have to remind myself that the profits in my account are not all 'booked trades' – I haven't actually closed the positions and banked the profits – so I could relinquish some of the gains when the trades are eventually closed. Yesterday's experience with HDR reminds me of that. So far I have successfully avoided Waterworld and in fact have made a couple of good-sized winning trades since my EXL watershed. The stats above show that you can have six losers in a row and a win/loss ratio of not much better than half and still make decent money.

## What have I learnt?

- I tend to get complacent with winning trades. It is just as important to check the closing price action for signs of a reversal when there is good money in the position as it would be in less favourable circumstances. If I'd done this with HDR, I would have avoided the big gap down and resulting loss.

- I am addicted to trading, and one of the reasons I don't learn from my mistakes is that I engage in certain trading behaviours compulsively. The trading diary is one way of highlighting these addictive behaviours. It's hard to beat an addiction if you don't even know you've got it.

## Do's and don'ts

- Do pay attention to the conversations of average investors. When a stock, market or sector is being talked about, it might mean that the horse has bolted, but, alternatively, it could mean a sector or company is experiencing a speculative bubble. This is a good time for short-term traders to trade, because this is often when the largest and fastest gains are made.

- Don't let yourself 'go on margin call'. That is, don't get to the point where your losses are so large your CFD provider requires you to recapitalise your account, or in other words, always use a stop-loss order. Waiting to go on margin call is not the same as using a stop-loss order. I don't do it now, but in my early days of being a part-time CFD trader I went on margin call once. I chose to fund the trade instead of closing it out, but eventually I had to exit and I felt like a big loser.

- Don't let your understanding of the big picture override the price action of individual stocks on the market. If you feel bearish about property, but housing stocks are rallying, heed the price action and not the noise.

## Lingo and lessons

### Account balance as a reflection of selfworth

A couple of months ago I attended a Supertrader weekend run by my trading coach for some of the traders he coaches. One trader mentioned that he had recently made $100,000 in a day. A few years ago he had had an ordinary job, earning an ordinary wage. His claim stuck with me, not because $100,000 is an extraordinary amount to make in a single day by anyone's terms, but because I couldn't even conceive of such success. For me it wasn't even in the realm of possibility. Was it because I didn't think I believed it to be possible, or because I didn't believe I would ever be good enough to make that much money? When I actually visualise myself making that much money I feel scared. To make $100,000 I would have to have the price of a house on the line.

## Addiction

I have an addictive personality. Most things that are addictive are bad for you and will eventually have to be given up. Your worst trading habits are addictive, that's why they are habits. If you keep losing money doing the same thing, (in my case, for instance, it's shorting into a bull market and adding too quickly to positions), eventually you'll lose so much money you will be forced either to give up trading or to change your approach dramatically.

# Trading tip no. 6

## Be wary of bearish chart patterns in a bull market

If you see a bearish charting pattern in a bull market there are two things you should know. First, it is less likely to be confirmed than a bearish pattern forming in a bear market. Second, it is also less likely to go to target than a bearish pattern in a bear market. You should exercise extra caution when scaling in, taking profits, and trailing stop-loss orders when you are acting on a bear pattern in a bull market. Similarly, a bullish pattern in a bull market is more likely to be confirmed than a bearish pattern and more likely to overshoot the initial target of the pattern. On the Arc Energy (ARQ) chart below, the double top pattern is confirmed but does not move to target before reversing and rallying again.

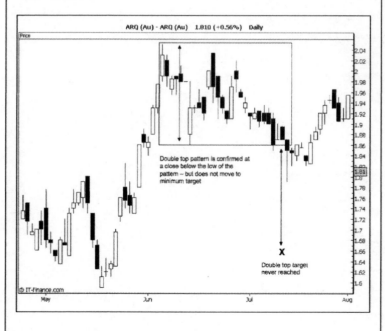

© IT-Finance

# Week 7

## My $10,000 week

## Day 30

Monday, 8 August
Total: $17,125, US$523

---

At 5.30 pm I go to my hypnotherapy session. The therapist asks me questions to see if I still have emotional responses to situations or memories she uncovered in past sessions. Unfortunately there is still stuff there to clear.

An hour later I call my trading coach for our weekly session. 'Attack and defence' is his mantra. Attack is adding aggressively to winning positions and defence is not letting winners turn into losers or allowing a small loser to become a big loser. My trading coach says traders must learn to access their superconscious state – the place where the inner nudge beyond what is logical, the intuitive insight, can be brought to consciousness and acted upon. He finishes the session with the line 'Your success is directly related to your focus.' In every other career endeavour I have managed to succeed without much focus, but with trading it is increasingly becoming clear that I can't get away with a similarly casual approach.

The intensive regime I've embarked on to turn myself into a successful trader reminds me of the reality TV show *Faking It*. The show takes people and trains them intensively for a month to do something that they have never thought of doing (or wanted to do) before – they might make a factory worker into a fashion designer, a housewife into a TV reporter, a chess nerd into a football coach. These people then have to perform against real fashion designers, TV reporters or football coaches in front of a panel of judges – seasoned professionals who have no idea which one of them is a fraud. More often than not, the judges cannot guess who is the real thing and who is not. If my quest to be a successful CFD trader was a reality TV show I think I could have convinced a few seasoned professionals by now but I still feel a bit like a fraud. Maybe it's not a bad thing because this feeling might keep me humble enough to stay out of Waterworld.

I notice today that even my losing trades are becoming smaller and less frequent. When you're in the zone everything seems to go right. I closed out a position on Arc Energy (ARQ) that has been messing around, not doing much. I lost just $131 on the trade. I closed my Coles Myer (CML) position, too, when I saw it break short-term support. I made over $600 profit on it. Part of my exit strategy for winning positions is to look for support levels forming on 5-minute charts. When the position is new, I usually let the price go lower by two support levels. I identify the first support level at the previous high in the rally. I identify the second support at the low of the most recent pullback. When the position is a long way in the money, especially if it has moved higher very quickly, I'll move the stop to a point just below the most recent support level or a resistance level that has the potential to become support.

# Day 31

Tuesday, 9 August
Total: $18,592, US$495

---

Before I started trading for the book, my coach told me I had a tendency to overtrade, so days like today are good. I don't take a single new position and my account balance is still growing. I close out 3000 Excel Coal (EXL), leaving 1500 open as the stock gives back 20¢ of the gains. I make $540. I take a loss of $190 on Newcrest Mining (NCM). I still have another 1000 NCM open. I have discovered that if I add to positions at different prices, it is best to leave staggered stop-loss levels, especially if the stock is not looking toppy. This is consistent with my trading coach's recommendation to stay in a trade, even if you only maintain a small position, to keep focused, so that you will be quick to take advantage of the next potential move higher.

# Day 32

Wednesday, 10 August
Total: $21,723, US$607

An ex-boyfriend comes over today. He visits me when he's bored. He lives with his parents in their large waterfront home and is currently contemplating his next career move, which means he's unemployed. His mother is having a bridge party and he doesn't want to hang around at home. He parks himself on the sofa in my trading room. After glancing at one of the charts on the screen he tells me the stock looks like it is consolidating for a move higher. 'I'm short,' I tell him.

I start on my favourite topic of gold and gold stocks. This particular ex-boyfriend was a gold trader for a bank in the late 1980s. There is no-one more bearish on gold than an institutional precious metals trader from the 1980s or 1990s. These guys were trying to trade their way through a dead market. Gold topped in 1980 when it traded above US$800, and then entered a bear trend, finally making a low in 1999, followed by a 'dead cat bounce' back to lows in 2001. (Dead cat bounce is an awful metaphor describing a falling market that makes a fast yet unsustained reversal to the upside.)

Once upon a time, when I first became interested in trading, this ex-boyfriend and I were a couple. We decided to get an office and start trading together. This was the second time we'd tried to run a business together; the first had already killed all the romance. The trading venture lasted a few months, until he couldn't hack the losses.

I persevered for a while on my own, but without someone sharing costs the overheads were too high. Back then live market data was costly. I left with some profits, but went back to full-time work. I traded while I worked and lost all the money I'd made and more.

# Day 33

Thursday, 11 August
Total: $26,041, US$1036

I close five positions today. The biggest win is on Aristocrat Leisure (ALL). I make $2600 on a single long position of 2000 share CFDs. This stock is a volatile one and it has been a while since I've had a win on it. Therefore I've been hesitant to add. I managed one extra position for 2000 share CFDs yesterday for a profit of $350. The best thing about this ALL trade is that I exit very close to the high of the uptrend, not because of any great higher knowledge, but simply because I've been running an ever tighter stop-loss level. I trail my stop-loss order ten times before I am stopped out. I exit at $13.75 after it tops at $13.85.

Trailing your stop-loss is also a much smarter exit strategy than exiting at market, especially with very volatile stocks such as ALL and Caltex (CTX). When a stock nears the top of a huge rally, it is likely to show very thin market depth; that is, there are limited buy and sell orders in the market. With many traders sitting on large profits after a long run higher, there is a great deal at stake; many are desperate to exit without giving back significant gains. Every move one cent higher or lower is crucial, because professional traders who scale in are now heavily exposed, and, as a result, even a small move down has a dramatic effect on the bottom line of their trades. Protection of profit therefore becomes paramount.

To illustrate, let's say in the recent trade I'd waited for ALL to trade at $13.75 before I decided to sell at market. The next bid in the market was $13.70, and a second later the spread widened to $13.65–$13.75. There were probably a number of other traders watching the price drop and wanting to sell at market. They would also be trying to 'get filled' at the best available bid price. The chances of slippage in this sort of scenario are high, and I expect I could easily have given back 10¢ ($200 profit) by using a market order instead of having a stop-loss order in place.

# Day 34

Friday, 12 August
Total: $24,813, US$1073

---

Gold rallies nearly US$9 overnight and my spot gold position is now showing a profit of over US$1000. After yesterday's remarkable jump in my account balance I have two things on my mind. The first is that Waterworld might be around the corner again. I can already feel a kind of complacency creeping in. The second is that I think I feel guilty about having made so much money so quickly. I ate pizza with a friend last night and paid for both of us. Today I take an impoverished glamorous flight attendant friend to lunch and foot the bill for that, too. I go shopping after lunch and I nearly buy an Italian angora coat for $650. A few weeks ago I wouldn't have even bothered to try it on. It's really hard not to tell the world I've made a lot of money, but I'm just as forthcoming when I'm losing, so maybe it's not just a skite. Still, in an ideal world I wouldn't be telling anyone. Your average person does not want to hear that someone else made $10,000 last week, even if it's an unusual event.

I start the day long 6000 Excel Coal (EXL), having added 1500 just before the close yesterday. I am variously set at $7.40 for 1500 (my original position established on 27 July), another 1500 at $7.66 (added on 9 August), and another 1500 at $7.79 (added on 10 August). Usually a strong close on EXL is followed by a gap higher and more gains. However, today the price for EXL opens down 20¢. I am stopped out at $7.95 on the last parcel of 1500 I added, losing $375. I move a stop for the remaining 4500 to just below the last rally high of the uptrend. This is a good place to trail a stop-loss, because the price will often find support at old resistance levels. Before yesterday's rally, this level had been the high for the month. My idea proves to be a good one when the price rebounds directly off that high, leaving me with my remaining position still open.

When you see price action doing something you expect, you can safely assume that there's a chance it will continue to behave in this way, so when I see the EXL rebound at exactly the level I had hoped and expected it would, I assume it will continue to rise and decide to add to the position again. My trading coach always tells me that if you get stopped out and the price action then moves back in your direction, you should get back in.

I wait for some consolidation action above the rebound level and then buy on a break of minor resistance. I get set for another 1500 EXL share CFDs at $7.06. That brings my position back to the same size it was at the start of the day – 6000 share CFDs.

In the old days, I would have beaten myself up for not widening my stop and keeping the 1500 EXL parcel that I was stopped out of. These days I don't care, and am happy to re-enter when I am wrong. I don't think about the fact that I've taken an unnecessary loss. I look at it like this: what if the price had continued lower? I would have been glad to get out at the level I did. The fact is we never know if a stock will go up or down and all we can do is protect ourselves from the worst scenario.

---

### The story so far

Profit/Loss to date – $11,813 profit

### This week

Closed positions – 21; Open positions – 16
Winners – 16; Losers – 5; Win/loss ratio – 0.76
Biggest loss – $404; Biggest win – $2516
Number of consecutive losing trades – 3

---

My cumulative returns from trading mean I'm now up more than 100% on my initial investment. I added nearly $10,000 to my trading account this week. If there was ever a time for me to slide into Waterworld it is surely now. However I have a couple of open positions showing a very healthy profit, so I know I have a good base from which to enter next week's trading session.

I have been reminded this week of the importance of leverage: if I were trading physical shares, with the measly $13,000 I had when I started, I couldn't even afford to buy 2000 EXL, let alone add 2000 parcels of ALL. Buying 2000 ALL shares at the current rate of $11.30 in the traditional share market without the benefit of leverage would require a capital outlay of $22,600. In comparison, my CFD broker has a margin requirement of 5%, which equates to an outlay of just $1130.

## What have I learnt?

- This week showed me it's a good idea to protect a position by getting out, waiting for the price action to give decisive direction, then getting back in when it does. It's better to stay out in times of uncertainty than risk a loss.

- It seems that when I am in the zone my losses get smaller and my wins get bigger at the same time. If this is true, the key to managing my account in a losing streak must be to work tighter stops and lose less. The question is – do I have the discipline to do that?

- Scaling-in – pyramiding into a position – is the smartest thing I can do. There is no other way to make the kind of exponential returns I have made this week. It is not possible with traditional share trading, either.

- Staggered stop-loss levels on pyramided positions are working for me so far. This technique is something to experiment with.

## Do's and don'ts

- Do add to positions when they are winning, but work a tighter trailing stop-loss as they continue to move into profit.

- Don't tell others about your big wins in the market. It might jinx it and it's not polite conversation.

# Lingo and lessons

## Slippage

The difference between your nominated stop-loss level and the price at which your order is actually executed can vary. When the stop order is filled at a worse price, slippage has occurred. The chance of slippage increases with stocks which are trading with high volatility and low liquidity.

## Expectations versus reality

When you don't have set opinions on the market, it's easier to take advantage of opportunities as they arise without emotion. When I was stopped out of my last pyramided trade on EXL I knew there was a fifty-fifty chance the price action could continue lower or go back up, but I needed to set some parameters around those two possibilities, identifying the particular level I would sell the remainder at if it fell, and the level I would buy at if it rallied. That's what the charts give me – the chance to determine the level at which I will re-enter the market or exit the rest of the position. This approach puts into practice The Director's ideas about not having an opinion.

## Execution of stop-loss orders

There is an important difference in the way that stop-loss orders are executed by different CFD providers, and this difference will have a direct effect on your bottom line. Some providers base the execution of the order on the course of sales data on the ASX: a trade-by-trade history of order execution which includes the volume traded and the exact time of execution. Course of sales data is a feature of most live trading packages, but if your trading platform doesn't give you access to it, you can ask your CFD provider to recap the traded prices at the execution of your order to determine if you are being fairly filled. Imagine, for instance, that you have a sell stop-loss order for 1000 shares of NCM at $17.00. If the stock trades at $17.00 for 500 shares, then at $17.01 for 1000 shares, and the price continues to trend even higher, your order will not be filled. This is because the full volume on your stop-loss order cannot be filled at or under your nominated price level. With another CFD provider, your 1000 lots sell stop-loss order may be half-filled at your stop level of $17.00; the other half would then remain open until another parcel of 500 is offered at this same price.

I believe some CFD providers give better fills on stop orders than others. You can compare the difference by checking the course of sales data. Stop-loss orders with some CFD providers are not true stop-loss orders. When your level is triggered, you join a queue system which means you may not get filled at all as the market continues against you. Some providers will charge to place stop-loss orders and this is a big disincentive to trail your stop-loss order.

## Overtrading

Overtrading is a common problem for beginners and can recur any time you fall into the cycle of desperation. Choppy, directionless markets often have me throwing myself at trades. In hindsight, trading these markets is like trying to trade shadows on the wall. The market is likely to be choppy after a prolonged period of trending or a short period of large gains, and in these conditions the chance of overtrading increases. Personally I find I overtrade after I've had a good run of profits and I take a few losses. Hoping to return to big wins, I start trading less significant opportunities.

# Trading tip no. 7

## Trailing stop-loss order strategy

The more profitable a trade, the tighter I work my stop-loss order. When I buy on an initial break-out from a chart pattern, I work a stop-loss below the low of that bullish pattern. As the trend continues higher, I will trail the stop-loss order as new resistance and support levels form on the chart. Mid-trend, I will use the second-to-last support level (S2), and when I think the trend is looking over-extended or near its end, I work a stop based on the nearest support level (S1). This works on intra-day, daily or weekly charts – whichever time frame you happen to trade.

© IT-Finance

The chart opposite shows the daily Aussie 200 index with support levels marked. When a chart looks like this, I would move a trailing stop-loss level to a point just under the second-to-last support level (S2). As the position moves further into profit, I would trail the stop-loss order to the last support level (S1). Note that in the Aussie 200 chart, the S2 level is an old resistance level from June, which turned into a support level in August. S3 and S4 represent lower support levels further away from the price action.

# Week 8

## Subliminal messages

## Day 35

Monday, 15 August
Total: $25,041, US$874

---

I exit three trades today, because my short positions aren't looking so good after the market came back with last week's rampant rally. I make $724 on BlueScope Steel (BSL) (after having seen the position up over $1400 last week), and take a small loss on part of my Newcrest Mining (NCM) position. Another Monday on which I don't open a single new position.

I'm burnt by Ventracor (VCR) again, and it's on a position I'd added to. I bought twice in one day last week, once at $1.33 and again at $1.42. While my winning trades were blazing a trail higher, I was ignoring the slow decline in the share price of this stock. I get out today at $1.30 and $1.29. I take a loss of $750 on the cumulative position. It feels like a step into Waterworld.

The good news is that, despite the losses, my account balance moves lower by only a small amount today.

A journo mate hangs out in my trading room for the afternoon session. He pulls out a list of junior gold stocks given to him by a gold mining friend. I check the charts; some of them look good. Once upon a time I was a keen 'penny dreadful' investor. The attractive thing about penny shares is the leverage. A 5¢ stock can move 10¢ or 20¢ like lightning, while blue-chip stocks might take years to trade at double or triple their starting price – if they ever do. Since I started trading CFDs, though, the attraction of penny stocks has diminished.

The Director says that it always amazes him when people reason that, historically, they have done well at trading penny dreadfuls, and so start trading CFDs with penny stocks. 'This approach is fundamentally flawed,' he argues. 'Clients think they can buy a penny dreadful and if it falls it will always come back to its value, but it won't necessarily. CFDs are best used to trade liquid stocks that you can get into and out of easily. These penny dreadful traders think that stocks like BHP are too expensive in comparison; that they can't afford to trade them, but CFDs were not designed to trade penny dreadfuls. If you're interested in trading penny dreadfuls, stocks worth only 20¢ to 30¢, stick to shares – you won't get a margin call.'

CFDs let you trade decent-sized stocks and get the same bang for your buck as you would trading a penny dreadful stock, but with much less risk. In my portfolio of around ten penny dreadfuls, there are two companies that have been taken off the board, which means my initial investment in them has effectively gone to zero. Although a blue-chip stock can be removed from the board, the chance of that happening is much less than two in ten.

At 7.30 pm I visit my trading coach for our weekly session. I tell him that I've noticed complacency creeping, in the form of not taking trades. 'You've got to keep walking through the door,' he says. 'I've got to keep you stretched.' My success is contingent upon taking trades – win or lose – so it wrecks my stats when I sit on the sidelines and watch good entry opportunities go by. If you want to trade for a living, you have to keep walking through the door, even when you think you're sitting pretty on a lot of profits. At this point I realise trading really is like a proper job.

Ashley J tells me that salespeople talk about 'hit rates' – a salesperson who knocks on ten doors knows that on average, the result will be three yes's and seven no's. The same theory works with trading.

# Day 36

Tuesday, 16 August
Total: $24,914, US$1066

Everyday I spend half an hour before the market opens checking stop-loss levels and analysing the charts of different stocks. As I turn on my computer, I also switch on Bloomberg television and catch the overnight action. I check overnight results for gold, gold stocks, and oil.

The correlation between the price of crude oil and the performance of energy shares is not always easy to predict in the short-term, especially if there has been a rally in crude overnight which coincides with a big sell-off in the US stock indices. The spot gold and gold shares are more correlated, but I keep in mind the fact that gold shares often lead the physical metal price.

The next thing I do is check the stocks I like to trade. I rarely venture from my list of favourites, although sometimes in the course of doing the Top Buy and Sell list for InvestorWeb I find opportunities offered by stocks I wouldn't normally trade. The following is a list of my most frequently traded share CFDs and some of my personal observations about them:

**Aristocrat Leisure (ALL)** – ALL is a bucking bull with the ability to move 50¢ in a day. I work wider than normal stop-loss orders on this stock and wait for more profit on the table before I add to a position. Anyone trading this stock should be prepared for the possibility of slippage on stop-loss orders and some very broad spreads – frequently 15¢–20¢. I generally open with a position of 1000 or 2000, depending on the stop order level: I choose 1000 if a wide stop is required and 2000 if the stop level needs to be relatively narrow. ALL frequently gaps on the open, though the direction of the gap doesn't always seem to bear any relation to the previous day's trade. In the current uptrend, a bullish reversal usually happens on a spiky looking low made in a day rather than a tidy basing pattern created over a few days or weeks.

**BlueScope Steel (BSL)** – BSL is one of my favourites. I jump in and out of this stock and make money fairly consistently, although it has been a while since I took a big slice (that is, over $1500) on a scaled-in position. This stock's typical price action is a break-out on the open and then a pullback. Sometimes the pullback turns into a bigger sell-off and sometimes it recovers. Therefore, it's much safer to buy BSL on a break-out if it happens after the first half-hour to an hour of the trading day.

**Caltex (CTX)** – CTX is another zippy one that needs a wide stop. I have to see plenty of profit on the table before I am willing to add extra positions. It also has very wide spreads – sometimes greater than 20¢. A number of times I've seen it gap through a stop-loss level resulting in nasty slippage. However, when it runs, it can go like lightning, adding 50¢ or more in a session. It is also prone to gaps on the open and gaps between the 4pm close and the auction close.

**Excel Coal (EXL)** – I like to trade EXL because it trends well and I find it easier to predict than CTX or ALL. If it rallies strongly into the close, there is a good chance it will gap up the next day and continue to rally. It tends to make big moves over three-day periods.

These are probably related to the T+3 rule on the ASX, implying that it is a popular stock with short-term share traders. Once in an established trend, EXL tends to give back very little, so I am rarely stopped out of scaled-in positions at a loss.

**Newcrest Mining (NCM)** – I tried to trade NCM intra-day for some time, but it was like throwing myself against a brick wall. I have been more successful trading this stock over slightly longer periods of a few days or weeks. NCM can have very thin liquidity and trade wide spreads. However, these wide spreads are generally triggered by a break-out, and the spread usually narrows again before the stock resumes trading with the trend in any volume.

After I review my favourite stocks, I compile a list of trading possibilities for the day. This list details my planned trigger levels, stop-loss levels and trade amounts based on these stop-loss levels. Today's list looked like this:

- ALL>13.08 buy 2000 stop 12.91 (this means that if ALL trades above $13.08, I will buy 2000 at market and place a stop at $12.91)

- BSL>9.77 buy 2000 stop 9.59

- CML>9.88 buy 2000 stop 9.70

- OXR>1.17 buy 7000 stop 1.12

I place alarms on my trading platform for all these trades so I won't miss any moves – a break-out trading opportunity can happen very quickly because everyone is watching the same key levels. As the day progresses, the possible trades on my list might become actual trades, or the trading conditions might change, meaning that new levels come into play. Sometimes I place an alarm on a stock at the wrong price and get in too late or too early; the worst case scenario is that I forget to set an alarm on a stock altogether.

I make exactly this mistake today. I don't place an alarm on BSL at the resistance level of $9.77. It sails up to $9.89, then back to $9.77.

I am making lunch for friends when it goes back to the break-out level, so I miss my second chance to buy. It closes the day at $9.87.

This is a good example of the break-out point or resistance level becoming support.

# Day 37

Wednesday, 17 August
Total: $24,911, US$753

---

Today I can feel that the mood of the market has changed. The sentiment around the rally high of last week feels like it's waning—the gains might have run their course. I look for cautious shorting opportunities but at the same time acknowledge that this is a fast route back to Waterworld.

I go short 2000 Coles Myer (CML) share CFDs at a break below support and get set at $9.65. Because I'm fearful about losing money on short trades, I work a tight stop, based on a congestion pattern that forms through the day. By the end of the day I'm stopped out at $9.68.

I also spot a short trade opportunity in my favourite baby – Excel Coal (EXL). I get set at $8.10 and sell another 1500 share CFDs at $7.91. EXL closes at $7.87 and I'm in the money. However, I suspect it might bounce back hard, so I'm already psyching myself for a very short-term hold. I might be out tomorrow or by Friday at the latest. There is a good chance that the day EXL reaches the ultimate low of this correction will also be the day it makes a massive rebound. I might well end up buying back my shorts and going long on the same day.

I'm revved up about uranium after writing two stories about it for InvestorWeb and talking to my flatmate, who thinks it's ready for another surge. I took a long position in Paladin (PDN) when I saw it trade a bullish daily range after a correction that had been in force since 9 August. I am now long 7000 share CFDs at $1.56. I'll buy some more if it moves above $1.69 – the high of 9 August.

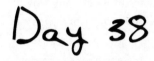

# Day 38

Thursday, 18 August
Total: $23,947, US$724

I'm at the bookshop today buying a copy of *The Great Gatsby* when I see a rack of subliminal cassette tapes at the counter. I buy one called *Create Unlimited Abundance* and play it when I arrive home. Instead of the sanguine American accent you would expect with something New-Age like this, the voice-over (the non-subliminal bit) is a man with an English geezer accent. He guides me through a visualisation in which I live in a mansion, step into my chauffeur driven limo and experience other grandiose moments of a pretend abundant life. As the tape plays, though, the accent makes me think of British gangster films or old guys selling fruit and veg on a grim London high street. It's difficult to feel like a disciplined trader when the voice instructing me sounds dodgy. Still, I like the idea of being proactive against

Waterworld, heading off the drama of big losses before they happen by being extra vigilant about negative thinking, so I go to a New-Age bookshop in the city with a friend. I ask the shop assistant for a tape on creating abundance. She directs me to a popular forty-day CD program. My friend glances at the picture of the author on the CD cover. 'Nice set of false teeth,' she comments.

I return home again and play the CD. First of the all the voice tells me that the program must be adhered to for forty days and not a day can be missed. Otherwise I must start at the beginning again. Then the author starts talking about the Bible and how God's grand plan is for me to be rich. Presumably this is to help cleanse me of any guilt I may have inherited from my Anglo-Christian upbringing. This time the narrator is American, but he sounds like the God from one of those epic biblical films like The Twelve Commandments. There is too much talk about God, in fact; I start to feel guilty and realise the chances of me doing anything consistently for forty days are remote. I turn the CD off before I get through the first session.

I add another parcel to my Newcrest position just before I close the whole position today. Sometimes I am in and out very quickly after pyramiding, as a new entry signal is given and just as quickly reversed on. When the price hit $17.28, I am stopped out of my original buy (1000 share CFDs purchased at $17.08 on 5 August); today's buy of 1000 at $17.51 is stopped out at $17.38. This isn't a great result, given that NCM has been as high as $18 since I entered the initial position. I think my scaling-in strategy might need some attention. I take a loss of $300 on BlueScope Steel (BSL). I'm short Caltex from $16.95, but I decide to exit near the close at $17.03 because Caltex can gap a long way on the open so it's a risky hold overnight, and it hasn't moved profit since I opened the position. I think this exit is a good move, when the present state of the energy markets is taken into account. Crude is trading over $65 and there are no signs on the chart that this rally has run out of steam.

# Day 39

Friday, 19 August
Total: $24,429, US$601

---

The dog walker comes to take small dog and my flatmate's old lumbering retriever for a walk today. She is studying postgraduate psychology, so we often chat about deeper things in life and not just what small dog rolled in on his walk. She also has a relatively new relationship with an academic and I always like to ask her how it's going. There's been a slow decline in her regard for him and today she tells me she plans to end it before it really goes bad. It seems the man is too independent and not capable of meeting her needs. As hopeful as ever, I ask, 'Why don't you see if he'll change?' It's the age-old contention – women try to get men to change and men don't.

As a trader, I think the idea of being resistant to change is ridiculous. The markets continually require you to reassess your opinions and sometimes to completely reverse them in a matter of minutes. If you don't change, you perish. The process of becoming open to change drags the very worst of your personality to the surface – your frailties and fears, vanities and ego, all in blaring technicolour – to be worked through and resolved. And this isn't a one-off event. The pain of finding out who you really are, and how much you need to change, is an ongoing and ever deepening process.

I think women are generally better at changing. The description 'getting bent out of shape for a man' is a common one, because it's something women do regularly. In some ways, it's not such a bad thing, because when we put our minds to trading we already know how to adapt ourselves. If you are reading my book and you are a proudly inflexible man, I don't believe you will find it easy or enjoyable to trade successfully.

Before the dog walker leaves, she tells me jokingly that experts have discovered that autism is actually a severe form of being male.

---

### The story so far

Profit/Loss to date – $11,429 profit

### This week

Closed positions – 22; Open positions – 10
Winners – 13; Losers – 9; Win/loss ratio – 0.62
Biggest loss – $575; Biggest win – $1380
Number of consecutive losing trades – 5

---

## What have I learnt?

- It's good practice to cut a non-performing position into the close.

- Cautious shorting is the name of the game in a bull market. You shouldn't get greedy with your exits and you should cut quickly if a stock starts to rally.

- You can't win if you're not in the game. Losses can make me miss entries, because I get too scared to step up and take a trade.

- If I pyramid into a trade and the price starts to reverse, I should not be afraid to cut the whole lot. Just because I have recently added to the position does not mean I am going to continue to be right. With a pyramided trade, there is more at stake.

# Do's and don'ts

- Do set alarm levels before the market opens and then continue to set further alarms at potential entry points as the day progresses. This helps maintain discipline in taking trades.

- Do focus chiefly on the price action when considering exiting a position, rather than thinking about where you entered the trade. As long as you have a stop-loss order in place and are trailing it higher periodically, the entry and exit points are unrelated. This is truly the key to trading in the moment, unswayed by opinion.

# Lingo and lessons

### Get to know a few stocks well

Before I wrote down my thoughts on my favourite stocks, I didn't realise how much knowledge I had accumulated about the way they traded. (Although I would never assume that they will always behave this way, or even that the next trader will observe in them the same characteristics.)

Setting out this knowledge systematically does seem to me to contradict what I have said about not forming opinions. However, I think my conclusions about these stocks are valuable, because they give me an extra feel for the markets I trade – a kind of instinct beyond chart patterns and fundamentals. Once you think you have passed beyond making silly mistakes (such as not working stop-loss orders), your instincts can take you to another level of trading. Relying on instinct is, in the words of my trading coach, 'being in your superconscious state'.

## Be a stalker

Getting to know a stock is one thing, but maintaining a relentless watchful eye is just as important – maybe more important. When you've had a loss on a position, your tendency is to walk away. The greater the loss, the more time it takes you to come back and give the stock another go, but if you are always on the case, it is possible to catch every single major move, and realise the right time to stay out. The odds of having a winning trade on a stock increase with every losing trade you suffer. Unfortunately your natural instincts are to walk away from failure. As a trader, you have to learn to love failure, because it holds the seeds of your next success.

# Trading tip no. 8

## A bullish daily range is a buy signal

I remain alert to possible reversals by constantly monitoring price action relative to the previous day. On the chart for PDN below, you can see that the last bar travels below the previous day's low, but does not breach the support level established earlier in the month. When the stock goes above the previous day's high, this is my cue to buy. For a more cautious entry, or if you are a longer term trader, you could wait to buy nearer to the end of the trading day, to ensure the stock closes above the previous day's high. This entry pattern has two key steps:

1. First, an existing retracement must be under way.
2. Next, the price must be seen to move above the high of the lowest bar of that retracement.

This bar had a lower low than the previous day, but rejected the correction lows from early August. When it closes above the high of the previous day it gives a buy signal.

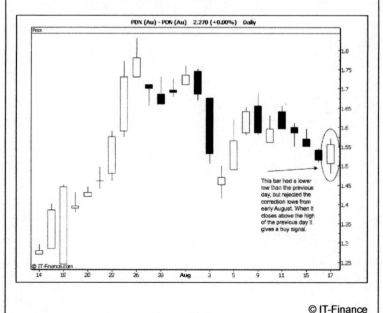

© IT-Finance

131

# Week 9

## Trading sucks sometimes

## Day 40

Monday, 22 August
Total: $26,160, US$643

---

On the weekend I go for dinner with accountant ex-boyfriend. He drones on about plans for buying his first property. I tell him to wait a few years and buy some resource stocks instead. 'Resources have topped, they're on the way down,' he counters. 'Fantastic,' I think. He was wrong about gold, so that means resources are likely to keep rallying.

The Dow Jones Industrial Index did nothing on Friday night, up just four points. More importantly, though, its daily range showed it rallied strongly, going as high as 10,626. It lost momentum as the day progressed and closed at 10,559. Movement like this is usually a bearish sign, indicating a test and rejection of the upside. The daily close for a market or stock is important relative to the day's price action. If the close is low after a largish daily range, it's a negative sign. It's even more negative if the market or stock has tested the upside, but then halted and fallen after meeting a resistance level like an old chart low or a Fibonacci level.

I also notice this morning that the US index confirmed a double top pattern by closing below 10,503 last week. With the Dow's clear rejection of the upside and the confirmation of the double top, I expect the US market might want to retest the downside; however, the local index had a good day on Friday and showed the kind of action that implied today could be to the upside.

I don't see any glaring short opportunities, but the outlook for the Dow makes me think I need to be conservative on my profit taking. I have an unscaled position in Pacific Brands (PBG), and I decide to exit it. I don't get out on my trailed stop but go to market in a panicked moment, taking a profit of $780. The stock does in fact dip, as I'd expected, but then it moves higher again. I've left money on the table and I don't get back in.

I have a conversation with David L. He tells me about a trader in the US who says he never exits a trade, winning or losing, except on a stop-loss order. David L likes the idea and I agree with him. The reality of trading is that we never know how much further a position will go into profit. It is also true that the chances of picking the terminal point of a trend are hopelessly small. Therefore, the logical conclusion is that traders should always trail the stop on a winning position, maximising the possibility of gains greater than those expected, while shadowing the market watching for possible pullbacks. I would add a caveat: the more profitable a trade becomes, the closer I place my trailing stop to the current price. A break of nearest support on an overblown rally is usually the first sign that a correction is under way.

I watch BlueScope Steel (BSL) run higher without me today. I hate being left out of this one, but I've taken a couple of losses on BSL recently and I can't find a good place for a stop-loss, so it's not worth the risk.

After the close The Director mentions that his CFD clients have had their biggest ever one-day profit today. I look at my figures.

My blotter says I'm up $2000 on the day – not a great result compared to some daily gains I've achieved in the last few weeks.

This too makes me think a big correction day might be around the corner. A market sell-off tends to come when everyone in the market is sitting pretty.

# Day 41

Tuesday, 23 August
Total: $26,636, US$705

---

After closing just under its highs yesterday at $10.09, BlueScope Steel (BSL) gaps down a whopping 40¢ this morning. I didn't buy yesterday, so I'm not caught out, and I'm glad. If I'd had a position open at my normal BSL position size, I would have lost $800. A gap down is not a good sign, so I look for a shorting opportunity. I get set for 2000 BSL share CFDs at $9.57. It closes at $9.62 from intra-day lows of $9.51. The rally for BSL has been hammering the upside since early July, nonstop. It needed to let off some steam and I think a lot of market participants with long positions will jump out. It's only later in the day that I realise what caused the fall – BlueScope Steel had announced record profits above $1 billion, but predicted lower earnings next year. As a technical analyst, I never look at fundamentals, but sometimes it's good to know I'm on the right side of the facts (for what they're worth).

I have eighteen open trades on my Excel spreadsheet trade log right now, and only one is a short. However, if any of my key stocks start to look weak, it's worth being cautious on the upside generally.

I bought JBM yesterday when it emerged from a correction on a double bottom pattern. I went long for 1500 at $7.93 and then another 1500 at $8.22. I take out half the position today at $8.39 after the stock fails to push through the early session highs and I work a stop for the rest at $8.29.

I add to my uranium position, buying another 6000 Paladin Resources (PDN) at $1.64 before it closes at $1.66. I'd been intending to add only when it went above $1.69, but I move stops in on the first position, so the potential collective loss is not too big. I'll buy more if it goes above $1.69.

# Day 42

Wednesday, 24 August
Total: $24,655, US$597

---

Today is nasty. The local market is king-hit, falling more than forty points before eventually finishing the day down thirty. I watch the ASX 200 open in alphabetical order and quickly see my well-nurtured Amcor (AMC) position smashed when AMC opens at $6.80, down 40¢ from yesterday's close. It is the BlueScope Steel story all over again, but this time I'm in the trade, and there is no lucky break. I've lost $460, more than my normal limit of $350, but the worst thing is that the position was showing a profit of over $1000 yesterday.

The local index is sold off and nearly everything goes with it. Paladin Resources bucks the trend, rising 4¢ to $1.70. I trail my stop and am out at $1.68. I make over $1000. PDN closes at $1.66, down 2¢ on the day.

I add to my short position in BSL, getting set at $9.45. It goes as low as $9.26. I work a trailing stop at $9.37, a cent above the previous chart low and am taken out before it closes at $9.40. It might sell off again tomorrow, but my new motto for short trading is 'Don't get cocky.'

When a stock has been in a fabulous uptrend and then suffers a correction, many traders hope to buy again quickly. This can create some wild swings to the upside, even when the stock ultimately travels a long way to the downside. This can turn a good-looking short position into a fast loser.

Of my nineteen open trades, I am stopped out of thirteen. Eight of those are profitable trades. Despite some nice profits booked – over $1500 on a pyramided Aristocrat Leisure (ALL) position – it doesn't change the fact that AMC is a big let-down. The Director has some words of advice. 'Trading sucks sometimes, but doesn't that sound like everything else in life?' he says.

# Day 43

Thursday 25 August
Total: $25,271, US$640

---

The Dow is down overnight, more than 80 points. BHP Billiton's (BHP) results came out after the local market closed. Although they were in line with expectations, it was sold off 3% on the UK market, where it is also listed. This means the outlook for the general market is bearish, as BHP is the biggest stock on the index. I remember The Director's comment that it is good to know what the average trader is thinking but be a contrarian. The obvious response in this situation is a sell-off, but a contrarian might see this as an opportunity to go long on some oversold stocks on the cheap.

I see Aristocrat Leisure (ALL) go as low as $12.63 on volatile price action – just the sort of reversal this stock usually makes when it's ready to start rallying again. I buy a tentative 1000 share CFDs at $12.88. I decide I will buy another 1000 if it goes above $13.00. I am watching my pager as it zips up to $13.05 over lunch, but of course I'm not at my desk and so miss my planned second entry. I walk along the road berating myself, so involved in the price action I don't notice I am talking aloud. A woman stops and stares.

Back in my office, I find that ALL has fallen back. I decide to wait for the price to break out above $13.00 a second time before adding to the position. Hopefully that should happen after 2.00 pm when the majority of traders are back from lunch. ALL is a crazy horse and it's up over $13.00 at around 1.30 pm, before anyone is back from lunch. I buy more. At the 4.00 pm close, its last trade is at $13 and then, at the end of the auction, it jumps to a close of $13.28. Last time it did this, it opened down by exactly the same amount the next day.

I feel like I take a convincing step into Waterworld today when I stop and reverse a short position in Jubilee Mines before it hits my stop-loss level. It almost immediately loses steam, takes out my long position, and continues lower. It is a case of getting spooked on the short side and not wanting to miss out on the long side. The old combination of fear and greed rears its head.

# Day 44

Friday, 26 August
Total: $24,012, US$587

---

A friend sent me an email. He's taken a margin loan for $25,000 and wants some advice. Investment advice for friends is a quick way to lose friends. I give him my general thoughts on the market, but try not to be too specific.

I told my mother to buy BHP Billiton (BHP) a few months ago and she lost $4000 in a week, but she didn't care, because she's an old hand. Widowed in 1983, she started investing in the stock market in 1986, mostly in penny dreadfuls. She lost a big chunk of her money in the 1987 crash when a lot of her juniors went off the board altogether.

Now she plays it safe, looking for high dividend return. She scours the *Financial Review* once a week and has a simple formula. She checks the share price against the dividend return and the earnings per share. She'll buy a stock if it pays similar dividends to other stocks trading at a similar price and its earnings are bigger than the dividend return. 'Usually if the earnings per share are much bigger than the dividend, the share price will go up,' she tells me. She gets out of losers fast – after only a few days if they go down in price – but she generally sits with a position for weeks, months or even years if it's going her way. Her latest favourite is Sims Group (SMS). 'It's up $4 from the price at which I entered back in June," she declares. "It's paying out 100¢ dividend on 200¢ earnings.'

There's nothing to stop a long-term trader using the same approach with CFDs, collecting the dividends just as a physical share investor would.

CFDs are a cheaper and more flexible way to participate in the market than taking out a margin loan to purchase shares. Both CFDs and margin loans allow you to use a combination of savings and borrowed money to take advantage of physical share price movements. The savings you put in become the 'margin' (or deposit). For margin loans the deposit amount is 20% of the value of the loan and investors actually take possession of shares (or a share in a managed fund). For CFDs, the deposit can be as low as 3%, and investors do not take possession of the shares, although they do receive many of the benefits of share ownership, such as dividend payments.

Many investors use CFDs to invest medium-term. It is like taking out a margin loan, but with the added benefit of being able to place stop-loss orders and guaranteed stop-loss orders, and cheaper borrowing costs. Share execution transactions on margin lending accounts are more expensive than normal physical share transactions, and therefore by definition more expensive than CFD trading.

---

### The story so far

------------------------------------------

Profit/Loss to date – $11,012 profit

#### This week

Closed positions – 26; Open positions – 10
Winners – 12; Losers – 14; Win/loss ratio – 0.46
Biggest loss – $671; Biggest win – $1025
Number of consecutive losing trades – 4

---

My balance reached an intra-day high of over $28,000 this week. Not a bad recovery from the days when it was as low as $8000 – in fact, more than triple my lowest balance. However, since that high I have been slowly losing money, and I gave up some of my profits this week. Losers outnumbered winning trades and AMC made a good dent in my account. Am I on the verge of Waterworld or am I already there?

## What have I learnt?

- A volatile week such as this is likely to leave me poorer – big swings in either direction can have me chopped up. If I see a couple of big days emerge it is probably better to stand aside or lower my position size until the dust clears.

- Big opening gaps can work both ways. They are heart-stopping when you are on the wrong side of them. I copped one this week on AMC and avoided another on BSL. If a stock has the propensity to gap, it is worth reconsidering positions at the end of the day. Moderate profit taking as a trend develops would help me avoid the next AMC event.

- My steadfast and exclusive focus on technical analysis is sometimes my downfall. Knowing the dates of general events such as profit announcements would be a good idea.

## Do's and don'ts

- Do keep a trailing stop-loss order in place, but beware that if you are trading a stock that has the propensity to gap regularly on the open, a gap open can wipe out profits in an instant.

- Do be aware of market news or profit results. This knowledge is very helpful in avoiding unexpected price movements.

## Lingo and lessons

### Rules for scaling-in

If you've never pyramided into a trade before, you will find it requires an emotional shift. When profits start to grow, our natural instincts are to pull the trigger to get out, not to add to our investment. However, when we are right, the chances that we will continue to be right are high. Therefore, when you feel that things are going well, and you start to think about exiting, this is exactly the time that you should be considering adding to the position. My trading coach says that without adding to positions, over the long-term, most traders end up breaking even at best.

When you are considering scaling-in, the big questions are:

1. when to add

2. whether to work a stop for each trade individually or for the collective position

3. whether to exit a profitable scaled-in position individually or collectively.

My approach, like the rest of my trading, is not necessarily consistent. At a course on money management, I heard Ashley J describe a simple scaling-in formula. He said a position should be added to when the profit on the initial position offsets the potential loss on the next scaled-in position. The stop-loss should then be trailed for the collective position. Ashley J admitted this was probably a more conservative approach than a more experienced trader would use, but since I don't have any rules about pyramiding, it is probably worth a try.

## Position-keeping blotter

The position-keeping blotter shows the user's positions with real-time prices. The position will either be positive or negative, depending on the closing price of the previous day. This is because my CFD provider runs a mark-to-market profit and loss. The bottom line in your account is based on the mid-price of the spread (the middle point between the bid and offer) for your open positions. This is necessary because margin requirements are based on real-time prices. This is the reason that a profitable position can be pyramided so easily: without the real-time profit and loss, your profits on open positions would not be credited to your account instantly.

## Stop and reverse

A stop and reverse strategy involves simultaneously exiting a position and opening another position in the opposite direction. The existing position is effectively closed by doubling your original position size, but by trading in the opposite direction. For example, if you are short 2000 CFDs, and you wanted to stop and reverse the position, you would place an order to buy 4000 CFDs, cancelling out the first position and finishing with an open position long 2000 CFDs. With my CFD provider, a stop and reverse strategy can be effected by placing an order at market for double the size of the open position. If you work a stop-loss order on the open position, that position must be filled on your executed trade blotter before a new position can be opened. Otherwise the new position you are opening will be offset against your exiting position and there will be no new open position in the other direction.

---

# Trading tip no. 9

## Fibonacci 38% retracement level as a barometer of strength

Fibonacci levels are the most complicated tool I use in trading and I only look at them occasionally. I specifically like the Fibonacci 38% level, which I call my 'barometer of strength'. This level is easily calculated by:

1. measuring the distance between a stock's last significant high and its low

2. multiplying this distance by 0.382

3. subtracting this figure from the stock's high for an uptrend, or adding to the stock's low for a downtrend.

For instance, say a stock moves from a price of $15 to a high of $20 and is then sold off. The total distance between the high and low is $5. Multiplying this figure by 0.382 gives an answer of $1.91. This figure is deducted from $20 to arrive at a Fibonacci 38% retracement level of $18.09.

---

In a strong bull market, a pullback to or above this Fibonacci level on a chart followed by a series of rising waves signals to me that the uptrend is likely to resume and take out the previous highs achieved before the correction began. The chart for CTX, opposite, shows that the retracement low in April 2005 was around the Fibonacci 38% retracement level measured from the November 2004 lows to the March 2005 highs. Note that the daily bar made intra-day lows below the Fibonacci 38% level, but closed higher in the range, demonstrating that the closing price is important, especially after the test of an intra-day low.

© IT-Finance

# Week 10

## Denial and regret

## Day 45

Monday, 29 August
Total: $22,700, US$557

---

There is a theory that when you're out of the zone, cars and appliances break down, clocks stop and accidents happen. On the weekend, my washing machine stops working mid-cycle.

At 9.20 am today I talk to my trading coach. He's moved my appointment to Mondays, just before the market opens. I'm still riding high on my success from a few weeks back, so it is a shock when I collate my figures to send to him and realised the drawdown on my account is looking ominously similar to my dark days of July. My number of losing trades also gives the impression that I have taken a definitive step into Waterworld.

'Don't anticipate, be patient,' my trading coach advises. It is as if he's read my mind. On Friday I took a trade on Excel Coal on a break of a minor level, because I couldn't wait for the more significant level, only two cents away, to be triggered. He says it is time to reduce risk by taking more certain trades and reducing my trades' size. 'Decrease impulsiveness, increase spontaneity,' he adds. I don't think I have enough experience of trading to understand the subtle difference between the two.

Mondays are starting to follow a pattern: there have been few trading opportunities in my favourite stocks on the first day of the week. I opened just one position today by selling BlueScope Steel (BSL) at $9.24.

I have been regularly drawing a cheque for $1000 from my trading account and leaving it on my desk, to remind me of my weekly goal. Each week I bank the previous week's cheque and replace it with the new cheque. Today I look for last week's cheque to bank but I haven't been able to find it. This is the worst of bad omens.

Before I go to bed I watch the coverage of the hurricane heading for New Orleans. The markets aren't reacting – further evidence that unexpected events have little effect on the market.

# Day 46

Tuesday, 30 August
Total: $22,696, US$206

---

I go short another 2000 BlueScope Steel (BSL) today when the price action breaks yesterday's low. I ignore Ashley J's rule and work a stop for both positions that will limit my loss on the combined position to $160. I'm out before the end of the day. If I'd worked the stop-loss level Ashley J suggests, I would never have entered the second position in the first place. His strategy not only minimises your losses, but keeps you from adding to positions prematurely. I realise that this is another common way I lose money – by adding to positions too quickly and then getting stopped out at a loss on the cumulative position. I probably lose more money this way than I do by just going short. Ashley J's way is never to lose on a pyramided position, but only to add when the cumulative stop will allow you to get out while still breaking even.

When I speak to The Director, he reiterates the point. 'The thing about trading is survival,' he said. 'You need to think about breaking even on every trade.'

The market makes a good recovery today. The XJO adds 40 points and regains most of yesterday's hefty losses. The chart for the index gives a good bullish signal. The low of the day is within a few points of yesterday's low, and this often happens when a correction is over or when a stock or an index is about to bounce. I expect tomorrow to be an up day. I run through my list of favourites before the close and I only find one safe looking buy. I take a long trade in Jubilee Mines (JBM), buying 1500 share CFDs at $7.74. It closes at $7.72.

# Day 47

Wednesday, 31 August
Total: $21,704, US$206

___

Gold drops more than $5 overnight and my supposed trade of a lifetime I entered at the beginning of July is stopped out. At one stage this trade was showing a profit of over US$1000, but I've ended up with a measly $270. I should be grateful I didn't run it into a loss.

There is something to be said for not making grandiose calls on the market. Never get too smug.

Despite the drop in gold overnight, Newcrest Mining (NCM) and Oxiana (OXR) hold their ground. If gold shares are leading the spot price again, then I probably exited my gold position at exactly the lowest point of the correction. I remind myself of the advice of my trading coach: 'If you are stopped out and the price action moves back in your direction, get back in. Never take rejection as the end. If you get out too early, enter again.'

I am still long OXR, and I see a promising basing pattern starting to form on NCM. However, with five losing trades in a row on NCM I'm a bit gun-shy. Still, I keep in mind my coach's advice. This is exactly the time when I should be ready to pounce – I'm due a big win.

The local index has been volatile, trading nothing less than 30 point ranges over the last three sessions, with a range down more than 50 points yesterday. Tops are volatile; bottoms tend to be the opposite. We could be in the throes of a medium-term top in the market.

However, by the end of the day, the local index tests the downside, rejects it and closes at its highs. If you were a casual observer, a close only eight points higher wouldn't be cause for celebration, but I have been studying the intra-day price action and see a different story. After spending the previous two days tracing out the same lows, it sold off today, ending with a rally into the close. I was more confident, and started buying. My favourite entry is BlueScope Steel (BSL). I like the trade so much I add extra volume to my usual initial position size of 2000 and get in for 2500 share CFDs. It closed the day a couple of cents higher than my entry.

The real news today is a big drop in my account balance. It's 3.41 pm now, and I still haven't checked my position-keeping blotter. I can't bring myself to do it. I don't want to see the damage; the calculations I've been doing in my head are bad enough. If a position is in the money one day but is stopped out the next, the loss on your blotter looks worse than the risk on the trade because it's based on the difference between today's price and yesterday's close, and not on your actual entry price. I'm in denial. It's foolish not to check the blotter – it's the only way you can ensure your positions are correct.

'You can't run positions and then ignore them if they are going against you,' says The Director. It always astonishes me when clients ignore their real-time position-keeping system.'

It seems I'm not alone in some of my bad habits. People often say that things can't get better until you acknowledge how bad they really are, but right now, denial is my friend.

# Day 48

Thursday, 1 September
Total: $23,029, US$206

---

Regret ... it's not a great feeling at the best of times, but it's an even bigger drag when you're trading. Yesterday I was stopped out of a trade which flew higher today. I was taken out of Caltex at my stop of $17.21 and the low of the day was $17.20. Today, at this very moment, CTX is back up above $18 again. It's sickening.

I speak to David L today. He likes Iluka Resources (ILU). I've never traded this stock before, and when I check it out, the chart looks gappy and the order book is thin. I ask The Director what he thinks.

He agrees with me. He opens a price depth screen on The trading platform and points out a lack of consecutive orders on the depth. When there are no buy or sell orders at certain price increments (levels), this indicates that the stock may be prone to gapping. Gaps mean slippage.

Finally, despite a lovely-looking congestion pattern that started to form in mid-August that is breached on the upside intra-day today, I decide not to take a long position, although it is very hard not to jump in. I remove the price and chart from my blotter to take away the temptation. The right stocks to trade are the ones in which you can safely manage a position. Of course, this doesn't mean the same opportunity couldn't be traded successfully by another CFD trader. For long-term traders holding for weeks or months, a gap of, say, 20¢ or 40¢ at the time they decide to exit a trade would not necessarily be a problem, because short-term volatility is not important to them.

My expectation of more upside today proves right. The bad news is that a couple of my favourites are going up without me: Caltex (CTX) and Coles Myer (CML). I watched CML flirt with a key level yesterday and didn't buy, only to see it gap through that level today on the open by 10¢. I baulked and it sailed even higher without me. Traders should forget the old cliché that says a gap is always filled. An old futures buddy of mine taught me the rule – always go with the gap. I didn't, and CML rockets more than 50¢ by the end of the day.

I am back on the case of Newcrest Mining (NCM) today, too, as I see my favourite pattern confirmation – a double bottom – after a correction lasting more than two weeks. I like the pattern so much I take an extra 50% on my normal position size and get in for 1500 share CFDs at $17.23 and I buy another 1000 shares CFDs into the close at $17.48. Double bottom patterns work just as well at the end of a long-term downtrend as they do after a shallow correction; however, I trail my stop more rigorously if the pattern forms in a mature uptrend than I do if a pattern forms at what I suspect are the beginning stages of a new uptrend.

# Day 49

Friday, 2 September
Total: $25,020, US$206

---

I am nursing another hangover of regret today. Spot gold rallied a massive $9 overnight. As I predicted yesterday, the point at which I was stopped out turned out to be the low of the correction. The best I can do now is get in again, if and when spot gold either pulls back or exceeds its previous highs. The latter option is more painful, because it will cost me more to re-enter.

There's a lot to be said for exiting a trade when the price action does not do what you expect, within the time period you had anticipated. When you trade on margin, time is literally money. Holding a long position that languishes costs you, because of the interest charges. Therefore sometimes it's better to scratch a long position at a minimal loss or gain, rather than wait for it to come good. When a stock does not move to plan quickly, it is often the first sign that your expectations are wrong. The big challenge when scratching trades is deciding whether you can trust your intuition, or whether you need to take a systematic approach. My advice would be to build your confidence in your ability to be disciplined before you bypass your rules and scratch a trade that is not performing.

Newcrest Mining (NCM) gaps up overnight but then falters. It makes highs at $17.75, tests them again, but can't go higher. I exit the position at $17.63. It has one more try at the upside, travelling as high as $17.69 before being sold off into the close, finishing the day at $17.40. I make a medium-sized profit on the trade.

My position-keeping blotter shows a healthy gain today of over $3500. These are mark-to-market gains, not actual closed-out trades. Nevertheless, my weekends are always more fun when I end the week on a winning note. This weekend, though, I have a feeling of dread. I can't shake it. When you've been in a flat cycle, or a losing cycle, the losses can start to feel normal. Even though I've made good money this week, it doesn't feel as though the tables have turned.

---

### The story so far

-------------------------------------

Profit/Loss to date – $12,020 profit

### This week

Closed positions – 17; Open positions – 13
Winners – 7; Losers – 10; Win/loss ratio – 0.70
Biggest loss – $445; Biggest win – $1011
Number of consecutive losing trades – 3

---

I didn't lose much or make much this week. I would like to think this has been a week of consolidation, and next week I'll be making money again, but I really can't shake the feeling of dread I felt at the end of the week.

## What have I learnt?

- I took a trade on EXL too early and lost money. Waiting for the definitive signal can be frustrating, but I have to remember that there's a fifty-fifty chance I'm wrong.

- Impatience has been my downfall this week: I have added to positions too quickly.

- I tend to put my head in the sand when things get tough. This compounds my losses, because I take my focus off the problems that need to be dealt with.

- Not every stock with a lovely large range is good to trade. The order book should be your guide. If the order book regularly shows a large number of gaps, this translates into slippage and is best avoided.

## Do's and don'ts

- Do exit a long position if a stock gaps open and then goes down. This gap is known as an 'exhaustion gap', and it is an early warning that an uptrend has lost momentum.

- Don't add to a position until the additional position's stop-loss level guarantees that the cumulative trade will not leave you with a loss.

- Don't anticipate, be patient. This should be a mantra for me and anyone like me who has the tendency to overtrade.

# Lingo and lessons

## Double and triple bottom pattern

My favourite pattern is a double bottom. Double bottoms can appear on long-term and short-term charts. (An example appears on the chart accompanying the trading tip at the end of this chapter. They might form at the end of a long-term bear market over a matter of years, or within a period as short as five minutes. A double bottom starts with a correction low, which is followed by a rally and then a retest of the original correction low. The price might either rebound exactly at the level of the original low or a small way above it. Sometimes the second leg might breach the lows of the first on an intra-day basis.

A third test of the lows creates a potential triple bottom pattern. The pattern is not confirmed unless the intervening high of the two or three legs is breached on the close. The minimum upside target for a double or triple bottom is the vertical distance or height of the pattern added to the highs of the pattern. However, this is generally a conservative target. A double or triple bottom often marks the start of sustainable longer term upward trends. For its reliability and predictability, I rate this as the best pattern to trade.

## Patience

Though it is a cliché, patience is one of the ideals of trading mastery. It is indeed one of the most important characteristics of a good trader. If you want to make money, you can't afford to jump in too early, no matter how convinced you are you've got it right. A short attention span and a lack of patience probably go hand in hand, and both of these traits make being a disciplined trader extra challenging for me.

## Bad habits

Beating yourself up over dumb mistakes is helpful if it stops you from making them again, but it's not helpful if it leaves you feeling like a loser. Loss begets loss in this game.

The important thing is that you don't let a dumb mistake turn into a bad habit. The difference between the successful traders and the ultimate losers is their inability to learn from dumb mistakes.

As a trader, I struggle with the feeling that I am alone, which is especially severe when I'm in a losing phase or when I've done something dumb. I try to remember, though, that when I was a broker, I saw people make all kinds of mistakes. You are not alone – every single mistake possible in trading has been made before and is being made right now by some other trader out there.

# Trading tip no. 10

## Corrections end with the double bottom pattern

The chart for NCM below shows a perfect double bottom forming at the end of a correction. The low range daily bars keep this stock off most traders' radar, but when it breaks above the high of the pattern it starts to move. The double bottom pattern is often the start of a sustained rally.

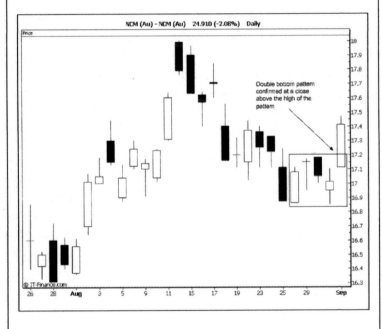

© IT-Finance

# Week 11

## Dogs with nine lives

## Day 50

Monday, 5 September
Total: $23,814, US$206

---

Small dog has a barking problem. He's at the front gate yapping triumphantly at nothing. I roll up the business section from an old weekend newspaper I've been keeping. I call him. He stops for a moment and glances back at me before he resumes barking. I approach him and hit him a few times with the paper. He cowers then slinks off. I unravel the newspaper and realise the irony – the story I was keeping is on dog stocks. The article, from April, is about a bunch of companies that announced lowered earnings expectations and were sold off dramatically. Some gapped, such as Paperlinx (PPX), PMP Limited (PMP) and Pacific Brands (PBG), while others, including Repco Corporation (RCL) and Housewares International (HWI), fell away with steady losses. It's testament to the strength of this raging bull market that this list of dogs has recovered and all are making bold moves higher.

They say the last stage of a bull market is characterised by increased speculation (and this stage could last for years). Wins on the board make investors cavalier, less discerning. Drug companies with nothing more than a patent can go ballistic, or the price of stock in a resource company with just a lease and nothing to produce can go up in multiples. It is at times like these that dogs get a second life. It's important to remember these days don't last forever. The more zealous investors become, the more vulnerable we are to a crash rather than an orderly correction.

My account balance drops $1300 today. It is a day of giving back profits, rather than suffering significant losses. I start the day short Aristocrat Leisure (ALL), am stopped out, see that my stop was just under resistance and then go short again.

Sometimes I set stop-loss levels without much thought, because when I enter a trade I don't really believe there is any chance the price will turn around and I'll lose. This means sometimes I am stopped out of a position too early. When I set a stop-loss, I should always realise that there is at least a 50% chance that it will be hit. Actually, when I check my hit rate, my stop-losses have a better than 50% chance of being hit.

# Day 51

Tuesday, 6 September
Total: $22,304, US$206

---

When I first got into trading seriously, I studied many different approaches. One of them was Elliott wave theory. I didn't get past Elliott's concepts of irregular flats and alternation, but I did pick up a couple of points that have stuck with me. The first is the idea that trends move in five-wave cycles, of rallying and falling. An initial upward wave (wave 1) is followed by a second, corrective wave

(wave 2), which may retrace all the gains of wave 1 (forming a potential double bottom). The third wave of an uptrend (wave 3) is usually the longest and takes the price above the highs of wave 1.

Another correction follows, known as wave 4. It is common for this fourth wave to terminate at the top of wave 1. In everyday charting language, this would be described as a double bottom pattern marking the start of a rally, with the highs of this pattern forming support for a correction occurring in the middle of the rally.

I've found this limited knowledge of Elliott wave useful in buying early after a retracement. However, today I use this knowledge to place a limit order to buy Newcrest Mining (NCM). After selling out a pyramided position last week, I have been waiting for it to retest the downside. With Elliott wave theory in mind, I have been looking for it to test the original double bottom pattern at $17.20. I place my limit order at $17.21 and it is filled, but the price continues lower. Knowing that NCM frequently overshoots levels, I place my stop-loss order under the lows of the double bottom pattern. It closes the day at $17.20 after going as low as $17.13.

# Day 52

Wednesday, 7 September
Total: $21,897, US$206

---

The ego trade – I do this today. I've been long Jubilee Mines (JBM) from $7.87 since Monday. I like this trade initially, because JBM has rebounded from a spike low made in mid-August. After the double bottom pattern, this is usually one of the safest signals around. It didn't do much yesterday and then today it starts to fall. I remove my stop, which I had competently placed at $7.69 at the time I entered the trade. I am thinking about last week's lesson – I don't want to be stopped out again on a stop-loss level I haven't thought through properly. Instead I move it to $7.51 which I identify as a cent below a $7.52 spike low in mid-August. Towards the end of the day I realise that I had this figure wrong and the stop is out by a cent so I take it off. The level I should have based it on was $7.50, which would mean a stop at $7.49. At the end of the day JBM is at $7.50 and I'm still in. Could you be much more stupid? It has been a long range down day, closing on its lows, and on the precipice of a major support line, a break of which would herald a major sell-off – a symphony of obvious negative signals. I would call this the perfect ego trade – thinking I know more than the market.

Learning to love your losses is a well-known trading rule, but it's not easy. I think there are two kinds of losses – the dumb losses you hate and the smart ones you can at least be at peace with, even if you can't love them. Dumb losses happen when you don't use a stop-loss, when you load up on a position in a volatile market, when you move your stop and get stopped out at a bigger loss, or when you make other similar, foolish mistakes. Smart losses happen when you place a stop-loss as you enter a trade, carefully remaining objective, but find that the market does the unexpected and that you are stopped out, incurring a relatively minor loss. If you make sure your losses are all smart ones, I think it's possible to love them, because they are the inevitable price of profitable trading.

# Day 53

Thursday, 8 September
Total: $20,553, US$206

---

So I have no stop on Jubilee Mines (JBM) and it opens down 11¢ and then sells off. I manage to get out at $7.30 – a loss of $1140, nearly three times my maximum risk amount. JBM finishes the day at $7.08. I don't go short because it feels like a revenge trade. My mood is bleak. I've lost a lot of money this week and feel like I'm in the midst of my second Waterworld. I have never consciously made such a ridiculous mistake on a stock and been so flagrantly undisciplined. It was the sort of error a complete beginner would make. That's the thing about trading: regressing into amateur mistakes is much easier than you'd think it would be.

Still, there is some good news today. My Newcrest Mining (NCM) position moves into profit. I buy another 1000 share CFDs as it clears a basing range at $17.25, after buying on a limit order at $17.20 previously. I now hold 2500 NCM. It tests the upside to the tune of $17.59 and then starts to sell off. My entry levels are good, so I hang on as it comes back and tests the downside to close at $17.38.

I'm going to start running a second trading account tomorrow. My CFD provider has given me a demo account to run simulated trades based on a back-tested system. I don't like indicators, and I'm a Luddite, so I ask Ashley J for his help. We choose to use a simple double moving average (MA) – a three-day period and a ten-day period. Why? Because we test them and find that, historically, they have worked. (If you want an explanation of MA or any other technical indicator or pattern, once again, I'd recommend John J. Murphy's *Technical Analysis of the Financial Markets*.)

'First of all we look for trending markets,' Ashley J advises. 'They provide some of the easiest ways to make money. (MAs work best in trending markets.) We decide which trending markets we want to trade by scanning the charts for stocks making new highs. Next we look at your usual trading time frame, and how much time you have left to carry out this experiment before the book ends.'

After testing a three- and a ten-day period on a series of stocks, we have a list comprising AMP (AMP), Coles Myer (CML), Consolidated Minerals (CSM), Caltex (CTX), Excel Coal (EXL) and Jubilee Mines (JBM).

# Day 54

Friday, 9 September
Total: $21,340, US$206

I take a lot of trades today – around ten, the most I've taken in a single day since I started working on this book. I'm cautious about overtrading. I take a revenge trade on Toll Holdings (TOL) by stopping and reversing from long to short. I incur a bigger loss than normal, over $500 on the initial trade and realise it's another confirmation that I'm probably in Waterworld.

I buy AMP Limited (AMP) on the open, in response to the back-tested system's signal.

I buy Jubilee Mines (JBM) again today. After yesterday's monumental screw up, I get back in as it makes a fast reversal. I manage to make nearly $400 before closing out. Before the session ends, I buy again. It might gap open on Monday. I congratulate myself on being able to get back on the horse.

---

### The story so far
------------------------------------------
Profit/Loss to date – $8340 profit

### This week

Closed positions – 26; Open positions – 15
Winners – 7; Losers – 19; Win/loss ratio – 0.27
Biggest loss – $1163; Biggest win – $451
Number of consecutive losing trades – 6

---

The JBM loss overshadowed everything else this week. Taking a big loss like that has perpetuated my losing cycle by sending me back into Waterworld mode.

## What have I learnt?

- The ego trade can strike at any time in your trading career. Even during the worst loss-making period I have gone through while writing this book, back at the very beginning, I never did anything as stupid as I have this week. The chances of an ego trade increase when you are feeling smug.

- Dog stocks can turn and rise savagely in a strong bull market. The lesson here is to be cautious about taking a long position in a stock that has shown a potential to fall precipitously.

- Determining my stop-loss level before I enter a trade is the smartest thing to do. It will tell me exactly how much money to risk on the trade, because the stop distance should be based on the entry point.

## Do's and don'ts

- Do set stop-loss order levels before you enter a trade. This is crucial to good money management. You are at your most objective before you have committed to a position.

- Do make sure that every loss you suffer is a smart one – not a dumb one. Smart losses are purely the result of price action. There is no avoiding losses altogether, but you can steer clear of dumb losses driven by emotional attachment to a trade.

- Don't be afraid of taking a position opposite to the one you have just taken a loss on. This is often one of the safest and fastest ways to make money.

## Lingo and lessons

### Moving stop-loss levels

Moving (or removing) a stop-loss order is one of the dumbest things you can do – second in stupidity only to setting 'mental' stops. Every trading decision has a fifty-fifty chance of being wrong, so the chances of a stop-loss level being hit are high. Make sure you set the stop-loss level before you enter the trade, because this is when you are most objective. Once you have entered a trade your attachment to the position grows. That's when those familiar trading emotions, fear and greed, run rampant. You cannot think rationally when you are experiencing one or both of these emotions.

## Mental stops are mental

I'm probably not the first person to say this, but mental stops are mental. Most members of this generation of traders have been raised on a bull market. When investing in traditional shares, these traders hang in there when a stock goes down, because it usually goes back up … eventually. When you trade CFDs, on the other hand, each move in the wrong direction away from your entry price is money out of your account. An actual stop-loss order is a real commitment to getting out of a trade. A mental stop is not. Using mental stops with CFD trading is a short trip to a margin call.

## Limit order is not necessarily the best entry

I always feel there is something especially hopeful about entering on a limit order. If you like the look of a market, why wouldn't you just get in? There are two things that worry me about waiting for a price to pull back if you are trying to go long or to go back up if you are trying to go short. My first problem with trading on a limit order is the chance that the price won't ever reach your limit level – and remember, the stock has to do more than just trade at that level. For a buy limit order to be filled, the stock has to be offered on the market at the price you have specified but also at the volume you have requested. Similarly, a sell order will not be filled until the stock is available at your bidding price and at the volume you have requested. Sometimes a price can trade continually at your level, but is never actually offered when you are trying to buy. My second problem with trading on limit is that you are essentially trying to enter a trade against the trend. Limit orders might only be a few cents away from the current market, but they are by nature below the market if you want to buy or above the market if you want to sell. Trend following is the easiest and most successful way to trade, and using limit entry orders runs counter to this approach.

---

# Trading tip no. 11

## Easy Elliott wave

Elliott wave theory is complex, but its most important principle is basic, and I find it helpful in identifying what stage a trend is in. A trend moves in a series of five waves: three waves in the direction of the trend and two waves that move counter to the trend. This phenomenon can be observed on the chart opposite. At the end of the final wave in the trend, the entire move is corrected. This correction comprises three further waves, usually identified on chart as a, b and c. This is one complete cycle.

The typical development of waves 1 to 4 is helpful to know, as I've found that markets often do conform to this pattern. Looking at the chart you will note that the termination of wave 4 comes back to test the terminal point of wave 1. This is a common occurrence.

You will also see wave 2 sometimes comes all the way back to completely retrace the distance of wave 1 (as represented by the dashed line). This is recognisable as a double bottom pattern. This explains why this pattern is often the start of a trend which will go much higher than the traditional target of a pattern, which is, of course, the vertical distance of the pattern added to its highs.

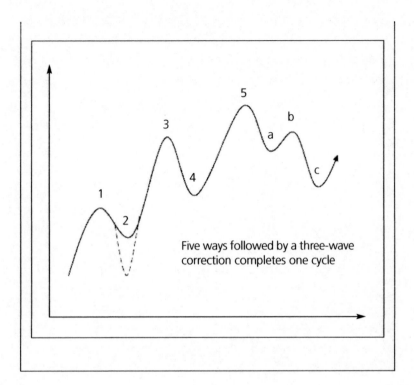

Five ways followed by a three-wave correction completes one cycle

# Week 12

## Golden sheaf

## Day 55

Monday, 12 September
Total: $22,552, US$206

---

There are three things I do when I'm pissed off with myself:

1. injure myself (fall down, cut my finger, get a bruise or suffer some other physical mishap)

2. shop recklessly

3. get a parking fine or other car problem

On Saturday I am returning from pilates when two garden sculptures catch my eye at a garage sale. I buy both for $90 and offer the owner an extra $10 to deliver them. He has dreadlocks, not the hairdo of the diligent, so I shouldn't be surprised when he half-finishes the job, leaving the base of one piece at the top of the hill that leads down to my house. I try to lift the piece but it is impossibly heavy. I have no choice but to roll it down the hill on the grass next to the stairs to my house. Inevitably, it breaks free, rolling away at speed, turning a corner and then rolling right on into the house across the way where my lesbian neighbours live. On hearing its thunderous arrival, the lesbians run out. One of them picks up the piece, as easily as if it were a twig, and carries it down the hill into my house.

One of the sculptures is a classical-looking woman carrying a sheaf of wheat – a golden sheaf could be good luck for my trading. I place it outside my trading room, but it does nothing to prevent the shopping carnage to come.

Later that day I find a padded bedhead with a kind of rococo border in a furniture shop around the corner. I buy it. I then go to the city and spend $180 on books – it has been a while since I've read a good one. Next I visit David Jones, in a strictly advisory role, to help a friend find shoes for her fancy new advertising job. Without a sniff, I spend $650 on two pairs for myself. If I'd planned ahead, a long position in David Jones might have been a good hedge. By the end of the day I have spent $1300. That's the equivalent of a profit in a good pyramided trade and more than three times my ideal maximum loss.

Having shopped to excess on the weekend, I'm not taking any risks today. Jubilee doesn't gap higher on the open, so I decide to scratch the trade mid-morning and take a one cent loss. Last week's mega loss on this stock has made me wary, and helps nudge me out before I can give back any profits.

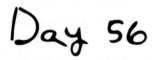

# Day 56

Tuesday, 13 September
Total: $22,124, US$206

---

I change my session time with my trading coach to 9am this morning. I show him my results for the week and he says that they aren't too bad, that most of his share trading and CFD trading clients have had a tough week in a choppy market. He sees the Jubilee Mines (JBM) trade, though, and says, 'Oh Cat, this is the equivalent of three losing trades.' He's right. I've already done that calculation in my head.

'You have a habit of building up profits and then saying "Bugger it, let's have a gamble." ' I hate hearing this so I know it's true. He then asks me how I've been feeling generally.

'Not great, a bit down,' I tell him.

'Let your feelings be your feedback on your risk management,' he suggests. 'When you're feeling low, it's time to pull back on your risk per trade; otherwise, you're gambling. What you're doing is self-harm, self-sabotage.'

He also reminds me of something I already know: when a sure-thing set-up like JBM doesn't work, it's often a great signal to take the opposite trade. These are the ultimate stop and reverse trades. Unfortunately, when you've been proven wrong on what you'd thought was a safe trade, and you've lost money, the last thing you want to do is jump back in straightaway. After a loss, your tendency is to go away and lick your wounds.

During the afternoon session, I hang out with my ex-boyfriend, the one-time gold trader. He looks over my shoulder at my screen as I explain a position I have in BlueScope Steel. I show him my stop level and he points to a gap on the five-minute chart. 'It looks to me like it wants to fill that gap before it goes back up,' he offers. If he's right, I'll be stopped out.

# Day 57

Wednesday, 14 September
Total: $20,862, US$206

---

Ex-boyfriend was right. This morning BlueScope Steel (BSL) fills the gap, I am stopped out and it goes back up.

One of the benefits of working from home is the ability to take naps. I take three today, only waking when the alarm goes on my computer, telling me to take a trade. Three naps in a day is a record for me.

I am in and out of Coles Myer (CML) and get set in BSL again when it continues higher. I also buy my uranium favourite, Paladin Resources (PDN). It has been a listless day on the markets and I feel the same way.

# Day 58

Thursday, 15 September
Total: $21,583, US$464

---

I'm talking to my flatmate. He thinks gold's a sell and he's ready to pull the trigger any day now on a short position in crude oil as well.

He trained as an economist, so being a chartist, I almost always disagree with him. He is bearish gold, reasoning that everyone is bullish gold, which is a contrarian indicator. To my mind, 'everyone bullish gold' means that my aunt, the neighbours and the taxi driver are all bullish gold. My flatmate only mixes with institutional traders and analysts, so I suggest that maybe his sample group is entirely made up of professionals and that their opinions are not a good contrarian indicator. Ordinary people are a good indicator. For example, I believe that we could be close to a top in the energy markets, because oil is making front-page news. Everyone's talking about the high price of petrol. This is the kind of contrarian indicator that works for me. Until gold gets the same attention, I think we are a long way off a top in the shiny metal.

# Day 59

Friday, 16 September
Total: $24,924, US$656

---

Gold rallies $5 overnight. I am jubilant, but also swearing – I exited a position in Newcrest Mining (NCM) yesterday, not far from the lows, and then watched it rally. It finishes the day at $19.45, around a dollar higher than the price at which I closed my position. The old feeling of regret again.

I'm on a date with a guy I met last weekend. He's Texan, and in Australia on holidays after finishing a stint as an investment banker in London. He talks at length, or actually throughout the whole date, about himself. I listen to a detailed history of his career, including his first job, which was at Enron. Unfortunately he was in a junior position there, so he can't tell me anything juicy about the fallen energy giant.

The Enron story is fascinating, and not unique to corporate America. It seems every few months a new big scandal breaks. It's usually a case of excess and fraud. I think these two factors are characteristic of boom times. I remember studying the activities of Alan Bond when I did my masters degree back in the early 1990s. The enormous size of the debts he ran up was a direct result of the banks' zealousness to hand over money. When money is cheap, as it is now, the system opens the door to many of the failures and scams that occur. The same thing happens on a personal basis with trading. I can get carried away with my own success and spend money carelessly or start to cheat my trading plan by removing stops or trading recklessly. As the date ends, the Texan tells me he likes my shoes. I tell him he should buy gold.

---

## The story so far

------------------------------------------

Profit/Loss to date – $11,924 profit

### This week

Closed positions – 17; Open positions – 17
Winners – 8; Losers – 9; Win/loss ratio – 0.47
Biggest loss – $467; Biggest win – $1469
Number of consecutive losing trades – 6

If only every week looked like this. My biggest loss was $467 – nowhere near last week's JBM disaster. A healthy profit of well over $1400. Overall, a good recovery from the steps into Waterworld I've taken in the last few weeks.

## What have I learnt?

- When the market is listless, I tend to fall into the same mood. This is not necessarily a bad thing, because it means I avoid taking positions when there are few good trading opportunities. The tough bit is finding the balance between staying alert to possibility and overtrading.

- Excesses, such as the events that led to the collapse of Enron or the Bond Corporation can also happen on a personal basis. When I'm feeling too rich or want some comfort from a loss I will spend money.

- Even hard and fast rules do not always apply. I believe in 'going with the gap' but sometimes it doesn't work: a gap may be filled before the trend has a chance to develop further in the direction of the gap.

## Do's and don'ts

- Do watch out for your own personal 'Enron moments'– don't get out of balance and give it all away.
- Don't regret the winning trades you take out too early. You shouldn't regret any trade that makes you money, even if you make less than you thought you were going to make. That's greed. The only mistakes you should worry about are the foolish loss-making ones.

# Lingo and lessons

## Filling gaps

There is an old saying in the market, 'A gap is always filled,' which means that the price will go back and retrace a gap up or down, filling the 'space' it has created on its chart. This is not necessarily the case in my experience. A gap is not usually filled within my trading time frame.

Each stock trades gaps in its own way. You need to study past price action to discover how important gaps are on a particular stock's chart and how they usually play out.

If you are trading off a gap, you can place your stop-loss just beyond the level at which the gap will be filled. Gaps are a good guide when determining stop-loss levels, because they represent important support or resistance on the charts.

## One bad loss can ruin you

Do not underestimate the danger involved in doing something dumb, like trading without a stop-loss or averaging down – buying at successively lower prices – into a falling market. Most traders who give up trading do so after making a single mistake that turns into a catastrophe. One big, bad loss takes time to recover from financially, because it can undermine your base capital. I've spoken to many traders who have turned one bad trade into such a large loss that they had to start from scratch and raise capital again.

The emotional price you pay for a huge and damaging loss is even more significant. When you take a big hit, it undermines your faith not only in your own abilities, but also in the whole profession of trading. Never let it happen.

## Other traders' opinions

While I like to read the opinions of some of the big contrarian commentators, when there are other traders around, it's better to tune out their opinions on the market. The most casual comment can enter your brain and have an insidious effect on your decision-making. Even if you think someone else is a better trader than you, it's wise to keep your own counsel. I've exited trades too early, not taken trades and moved stop-loss levels – and all because I've listened to other traders. I find I am more likely to seek out the opinion of another trader when I am subconsciously or consciously expecting a loss.

## Pattern failure

If you see a great set-up in the market and it doesn't work, chances are the reverse trade will be very profitable. To exploit these opportunities, I make a point of setting an alarm for the opposite signal, even when I'm glued to the price action. When the alarm goes off, it reinforces the trigger signal telling me to take the trade in the opposite direction.

If the original pattern gave a buy signal and there was a very safe looking set-up, you might find it hard to get past your bullish outlook and go short, but it is often worth making the effort. Pattern failure is one of the fastest ways to make a lot of money in trading.

# Trading tip no. 12

## Pattern failure: a 'stop and reverse' signal

The better the set-up for a pattern, the more potentially profitable a trade in the other direction is likely to be if the set-up fails. I should have remembered this when my trade in JBM went wrong last week. JBM had tested and rejected a major level and then formed a small congestion pattern, which is normally a great set-up for a buy. I bought at a break to the upside of this pattern, but the trend reversed rapidly and I moved, and then removed, my stop-loss orders. The basing pattern failed when the price fell below the low of the pattern, offering a fabulous shorting opportunity, but I didn't take it. This is the sort of situation in which a CFD trader should stop and reverse, as there is a high probability the second, reversed trade will be profitable.

JBM (Au) - JBM (Au)  7.760 (+1.17%)  Daily

Went long on congestion pattern formed on test and rejection of August lows.

Bearish signal – large range lower, closes on the lows, precipice of major support.

© IT-Finance

# Week 13

## Blonde psycho

## Day 60

Monday, 19 September
Total: $24,253, US$913

---

I'm in Melbourne to present a seminar for InvestorWeb. I've spent the weekend shopping – shopping away Friday's unrealised profits. I spent nearly $1000 in one shop alone. When I'm not losing money making dumb mistakes in the market, I find other ways to get rid of it, although a trip down Greville Street is an infinitely more enjoyable way to give away the bucks than lifting a stop-loss order at the wrong time.

I call the IWL office to check on the seminar details. I was expecting a small group of twenty to forty to attend, but they tell me there are nearly 100 IWL members coming.

The key to public speaking for me is to talk only about things that really turn me on. When I'm excited about a topic, words flow and the audience is mine. Talking about investing or trading can be dry, so another thing I do is make some big declarations. Too many commentators sit on the fence in this country; they don't want to be wrong and have someone say 'I told you so.' I started talking about gold going to $2000 or $3000 an ounce a couple of years ago, before most people were even game enough to call what was happening a new gold bull market.

So when an audience looks like it is waning, I talk about house prices dropping 90%, gold going into the thousands per ounce and the next junior gold stock going up ten times in value.

Talking about the idea of a housing collapse might be going a bit far, because there's a point where you can alienate the audience. Most people who attend seminars about share investing tend to be homeowners and often multiple property owners – they don't want to face the possibility of huge negative equity. Still, I reminded them of the bear market for housing in Japan in which prices fell 90%. Earlier this year, the first rise in housing prices in Japan in 17 years was announced – that is, the first rise above the low set by the 90% fall so long ago. How many years will it take for Japanese housing prices to return to the high of the late 1980s? The recent Japanese experience was the last thing on Australian investors' minds when they bought in the middle of a bubble in the early 2000s.

My view on the property market is derived from the old rule: when an asset bubble bursts, the correction usually sees prices drop by 90%. The best example of the 90% rule was the 1929 crash. The US market fell from a high of 396 in September 1929 to a low of 40.56 in 1932 – a drop of 89.5%. It wasn't until 1954 that the Dow Jones Industrial Index was back at its 1929 highs. This phenomenon is significant, because it tells us that a buy-and-hold strategy can be disastrous if you get your timing wrong. Just because buy-and-hold works sometimes does not mean it works all the time.

Of course the greatest number of investors join the trend when the market is already going crazy – that's how uptrends become booms and then bubbles. Speculation increases dramatically at times like these. Buy and hold is a crazy mantra pushed by people that never look at charts; inspite of this, it's become stock market fact.

When the stock market is in big-time decline, you can bet that the rest of the economy is also going to the dogs, and that buy-and-hold investors will need the money they have tied up in shares or investment properties. Bubbles turn to crashes, and when the smoke clears, a large percentage of stocks are off the board entirely. That's not something even the charts of indices can show us, because these stocks stop being counted in the averages when they are de-listed. I don't believe there is such a thing as a bubble followed by a soft landing. It goes against human nature.

Fast forward to the tech boom. Can you name more than a couple of Australian tech stocks that are still on the board? Most went broke altogether or were absorbed by other companies, but not before they had lost 90% or more of their values at the peak of the tech bubble.

Telstra (TLS) is in the news at the moment. It's another stock I have a fairly unpopular view on – I believe that it will eventually make lows beneath its initial subscription price. Why? For no other reason than the fact all the 'mums and dads' in Australia bought this stock. The market has shown me that when the majority of people are in on a stock or a sector, it usually ends up going down big time. That's not to say that there aren't many mums and dads who took the money and ran, but ultimately the majority will still be holding and crying. Actually the usual scenario is that the mums and dads sell out at around the time the lows of the correction are being made.

CFDs work differently: the downside need not be bad news. Your TLS holding can be hedged by taking a short position in CFDs. Having both the physical holding and the short CFD position means a drop in the value of the price of TLS is offset by the short position. Alternatively, an outright short position in a multi-year major downtrend like the one TLS has experienced can be ridden with low margin and cheap brokerage, and the added bonus of your CFD provider paying you interest while the position is open.

# Day 61

Tuesday, 20 September
Total: $27,133, US$900

---

In the taxi on the way home from the airport, the taxi driver asks me what I do for a living. I tell him I'm trading. 'If you're trading then it can't be that hard,' he says. 'I mean you're blonde and you're a girl.' I should be offended but I laugh. After all, I'm the one riding in the back.

I don't fit any stereotype of a trader, but I've interviewed enough traders over the last few years to know they are a mixed bunch. Serious women traders are rare, but my trading coach says we make better traders, because we don't have the ego of the average male trader. Still, I think women face another enemy. It's a generalisation, of course, but women in our culture do tend to be more emotional than men. When emotional issues arise, I think women have to make an extra effort not to take them into the trading room. That's been the case for me – and until I started trading I didn't consider myself especially prone to emotional extremes. Men are better at blocking out feelings and emotions, so I believe it is easier for them to leave their personal issues out of their trading. For men, the biggest problem in trading is their ego. What's easier to deal with – ego or tears?

I ask The Director about the emotion versus ego question. 'It's not emotion, it's the fear factor,' he said. 'A certain amount of fear is good, because fear leads to heightened self-awareness and increased mental processing. There are times when I'm on the trading floor and I can sense the tension building – for instance, when a big figure is coming out. You have to avoid being overwhelmed. If you think you might be getting overwhelmed, maybe trading is not for you. It's not about 'conquering fear', that's a made-up expression. It's about controlling fear. It's about putting fear in the box. I learnt to do that from an early age, probably because as a kid I was always doing mad things. If you allow yourself 15 seconds of panic and let it all wash over you, then you can go on again.

'Personally, I see ego as a far bigger challenge than fear. The problem is the urge to have an ego trade always happens after a really good run. You have the money in your account and you throw it away. It's a matter of finding the right balance – deciding how much money to keep in your account. My advice is to take it out before you blow it on an ego trade. It's like when you're a kid – you're given a bag of sweets and you eat the whole bag. Take the bag away.'

I think The Director is right. I don't know if it's possible to completely remove the urge for the ego trade, so the best thing to do is reduce its potential.

At mid-morning I take a call from a freelance journalist. He's writing a story about the stock market for a women's business magazine. He was given my name by a friend of a friend, but coincidentally, I've done some freelance work for the same magazine in the past. He wants to know about trading for a living. He asks me if I have a diversified approach. I tell him that the opposite is probably true: I go with the best looking stock and load up. If I'm right, that's where I'm going to make the most money. 'Is it like gambling?' he asks. I hate the idea of wasting money in a casino, so it must be different, but I concede that there are times when trading is probably not much better than gambling. When I'm feeling greedy or desperate to make money, I'm cavalier. Gambling and trading take you through the same gamut of emotions.

I explain the emotional element, tell him that being a woman can make trading more challenging. For instance, if you had a broken heart, it would be more difficult, because it's hard to trade well when you're sad. 'Are you making money at the moment?' he asks. 'Yes,' I tell him. 'My heart's not broken.' This is probably not the kind of quote he wants for a mag that's all about women kicking butt.

# Day 62

Wednesday, 21 September
Total: $26,132, US$1281

---

I read an article in the newspaper today that says the best investors are 'functional psychopaths'. US scientists have found that the emotionally impaired are more willing to gamble for high stakes and may therefore make good financial decisions. The study compared the performance of 15 people with lesions on the brain that affected their emotions with that of a control group. The people with damaged brains outperformed the normal brain sample. The scientists concluded the advantage of the brain lesions was less fear of loss. The participants with brain lesions did better than the participants who had not suffered brain lesions, even in situations where the potential benefits of a certain course of action clearly far outweighed the potential losses. The scientists named the 'normal' participants' tendency to avoid loss 'myopic loss aversion'.

I like this term. I think myopic loss aversion is something we suffer at times. When the going gets tough and I'm losing money, my appetite for risk is definitely affected. It might grow, sending me into gambling mode, or it might drop away in fear. When it drops, this is a form of self-preservation, and my trading coach would probably say it's a good thing. However, when you're in the zone, you sometimes need to expand your vision and trade anything in sight, rather than taking the short-sighted view and trying to avoid loss. I think good traders are flexible enough to know when to be loss-averse and when to bet the farm.

It follows that an inflexible or mechanical trading system is probably a disadvantage, unless it specifically has a money management element built around your recent cycle of success or failure.

Proof that trading can send you psycho ... in 1999, an Atlanta chemist-turned-day-trader by the name of Mark Barton killed nine people at two separate brokerage firms. The killings were thought to be related to Barton's trading losses of about US$105,000 over the previous month. He also killed his wife and children before killing himself.

Later in the day a friend telephones and declares me a psychopath. He's also read the article and thinks it's funny.

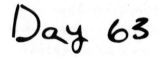

## Day 63

Thursday 22 September
Total: $26,385, US$932

---

Some days don't feel like money-making days, but you make money anyway. It's surprising, and I wonder how that works.

I am at the Sydney IWL seminar. I have a heckler. I tell the audience I took a trip to the gold bullion dealer earlier today to buy a one ounce bar of bullion. I asked the coin dealer about the typical customer. The coin dealer said he had a lot of Indians and crazy people buying gold coins and bars. When I relate this information, some smart guy in the audience yells out, 'Well you're not Indian.'

My gold play is diversified. I have a bunch of junior gold stocks that I accumulated between 2001 and 2003. Since I got onto CFDs, I haven't been as big a fan of these stocks. I have also bought a few coins and bars since gold started to rally in Aussie dollars in the middle of this year. There wasn't much point before that happened, because every time there was a rally in the price of gold, it was greeted with a fall in the Australian dollar. I like the coins and bars because they are pretty to look at, but they don't provide the best potential for profiting from this gold bull market.

The real guts in my gold play is CFDs – both share CFDs and a position in a spot gold CFD. With gold share CFDs, I can trade with twenty times leverage and no currency risk. For example, if I buy 1000 Newcrest Mining (NCM) at $20, the margin requirement is just $1000. Spot gold CFDs give me 100 times leverage and can be traded in either Australian dollars or US dollars. I trade spot gold in US dollars, just because this is the way it's most commonly quoted. As I am trading from Australia, though, this means spot gold has currency risk, unlike gold shares. A fall or rise in the gold price may occur at the same time as a fall in the value of the Aussie dollar, so when you convert your position back to local currency, you will make less profit or a greater loss than the move in the commodity price. The big advantage of trading spot gold with CFDs is clearly the leverage.

The other way for traders to get exposure to spot gold with leverage is through gold futures contracts. The minimum contract size for a gold futures contract on the New York Mercantile Exchange or NYMEX is 100 ounces, and at the moment the margin deposit per contract is US$1300. The margin requirement is routinely raised when the price action in the contract experiences increased volatility. A spot gold CFD requires less margin and offers more flexibility than a futures contract. I can trade as little as 50 ounces of spot gold with CFDs, making a margin deposit of just 1%. If gold is trading at US$460 an ounce, for example, and I buy 50 ounces using CFDs, my total margin requirement is around US$230.

# Day 64

Friday, 23 September
Total: $27,842, US$823

---

I telephone Doug Noland in the US for an interview. He's the subject of a profile piece I'm writing for *Your Trading Edge* magazine. A fund manager for the Prudent Bear fund, Noland is most famous for his column 'Credit Bubble Bulletin', a massive weekly essay on the state of the US and global credit or interest rate markets. I think he's a genius. For a stock investor or trader, interest rate markets might not seem important, but Noland is looking for cracks in the financial system. When the credit bubble bursts, he reckons it's not just interest rate markets that will be trouble. He expects stocks to get swept out of town along with everything else.

According to Noland, the manic growth in global credit – easy access to cheap money – has been driven by past financial boom and bust events, starting with the fallout of the 1980s' share boom. Part of that fallout was the collapse of the savings and loan industry and bank failures in the US. These events threatened the whole global financial system and economy. The Fed responded by aggressively lowering interest rates while government-sponsored enterprises (GSEs), Freddie Mac and Fannie Mae, started to push mortgage credit into the economy, aggressively expanding their balance sheets, fuelling the housing boom. At the same time, Wall Street started to create new securities: asset-backed and mortgage-backed instruments that also channelled more credit into the system. This was accompanied by a growth in the hedge fund industry, and a whole new world of credit creation outside the banking system was born.

In 1994 Mexico suffered a financial crisis, which was followed by more aggressive lending on the part of the GSEs. Noland says that as the Fed continued to lower rates, the hedge fund industry was encouraged to step up to another level of excess. This resulted in the collapse of the derivative markets in South-East Asia and the Russian financial markets, as well as the famous crash of the hedge fund Long Term Capital Management (LTCM).

Once again the Fed responded by lowering interest rates and the GSEs increased their lending. This led to the next bubble, which was in the technology and internet sector. The hedge funds got bigger and bigger as a result. Noland noted that each successive bubble was getting larger. When the tech boom turned to wreck, he forecast, correctly, that the next boom would be in the mortgage market. He thinks this bubble is now so much bigger than any bubble that has gone before that the Fed is unable to control it. Noland spends his days monitoring statistics and news, looking for a trigger event that could cause the latest bubble to burst. A derivative accident or a crisis in the US dollar are a couple of the possible events that Noland thinks may trigger the bubble's ultimate collapse. He thinks this could potentially leave the US economy in a 1929-style depression.

The funds he helps manage are long gold stock and have loaded up on safe government securities like Australian government bonds. The

Prudent Bear Fund is also poised to take advantage on the short side on stocks in overblown areas of the market, such as the retail, mortgage and service provider sectors.

The Director was caught in the LTCM collapse when he was working for an options broker. The volatility which followed made trading impossible. 'The lesson it taught me is that there will always be that big wacky event that will blow it all away,' he says. He remembers the day the planes hit the World Trade Center buildings. 'There was a 3000 point spread on the Dow.'

Instead of trying to predict a meltdown or trigger event, The Director suggests using my CFD provider's guaranteed order facility. A guaranteed order carries an extra charge, but you can specify that it remain 'good till cancelled', which means it sits in the market indefinitely until the predicted event happens. A guaranteed sell stop order will make sure your positions are closed at the level you nominate with no slippage in the event of a catastrophe and market crash. Guaranteed orders can also be used to close out short positions for potential rapid movements higher. However, the dread of a sudden fall is the real concern when you are involved in the share or CFD market.

---

### The story so far

- - - - - - - - - - - - - - - - - - - - - - - - - - - - - - - - - -

Profit/Loss to date – $14,842 profit

### This week

Closed positions – 27; Open positions – 15
Winners – 10; Losers – 17; Win/loss ratio – 0.37
Biggest loss – $509; Biggest win – $1772
Number of consecutive losing trades – 5

---

Nice gains this week – I'm back in the zone. It always amazes me that I can have a win/loss ratio of less than half and still make a good profit. This is due to a combination of pyramiding, leverage, and the fact that my CFD provider instantly adds profits from my winning positions to my bottom line.

## What have I learnt?

- A guaranteed stop-loss order is the best insurance policy you will find in the financial markets. I don't know of any other kind of broker – share or derivative – that offers this facility. I don't expect I will need it that often, but when I have accumulated a large, pyramided long position, it will be useful in protecting me from a big loss (on a gap open, for example, or when a company is due to issue results).

- The psychological impact of a loss is directly related to the sort of mistake you've made. A loss resulting from stupidity or lack of discipline is much more painful than a loss incurred when trading in a disciplined manner.

- Stereotypes are irrelevant in successful trading. Anyone can trade and make money, no matter what their background. When the taxi driver declared trading must not be that difficult if I were doing it, he only strengthened my confidence in my ability.

- Trading penny dreadful stocks is riskier than trading share CFDs with a stop-loss order, because they can potentially fall to zero value and go off the board. This rarely happens to top ASX companies.

- The JBM trade of last week has left a permanent scar on my trading psyche. It reminds me of a motto of an old trader friend of mine: 'Survive the tough times and you can play another day.' This is the most valuable lesson I have learnt while working on this book so far.

## Do's and don'ts

- Do stop trading and reassess your actions if you feel in any way as though you are gambling. This feeling almost certainly arises when you aren't trading according to your plan.

- Don't feel inclined to go shopping or make a large purchase on the back of profits in your trading account (or losses for that matter – it won't make you feel better).

## Lingo and lessons

### Booms and busts

I've observed that markets tend to make the biggest gains towards the end of a boom. That's the best time to make quick gains, but also the time the Johnny-come-lately's enter and lose all their dough. The later stages of a boom are also the time when a bull market can end quickly, so you should use a tight stop-loss and narrow that stop-loss level as the market climbs. When things get crazy, be ready to take the money and run. Remember the rule – when you start counting the cash, it's usually time to leave.

When the mainstream financial media start talking about the gains in a market, the uptrend is usually well under way. When the rally makes it into the general news pages, it's probably close to or at a top. When it's front-page news, it's likely that it is at the very top, or has already topped. Similarly, when friends who know nothing about the markets, neighbours, taxi drivers and strangers at barbecues start giving tips on a market, it's usually either close to or at a top.

Amateur investors exit when they have already lost a large amount of money, not when the market is overdone or spiking or blowing out. Amateurs usually exit a market after it has already bottomed.

If a boom and crash is big enough, it will wipe out a generation of investors – they'll be sworn off share trading for life.

## Ego versus tears

It's not only women traders who cry. According to my trading coach, he's seen some big, burly guys sobbing over losses. If you have a family and a mortgage to maintain, a large loss could easily make you extremely emotional. I've wondered whether it is harder to trade when you have difficulty controlling your emotions or when you are fighting a runaway ego. My guess is it's harder to trade with a big ego. The thing about ego is that most people with big egos don't know they have one. The power of the ego only rears when you are backing a loser to the hilt.

## Trade rage

To avoid going on a shooting rampage, you should take preventative measures to deal with trade rage. Stress and inertia call for a physical outlet. A few weeks ago I went to a meditation group and the leader of the group started playing this music and asked us to get up and dance around in the nerdiest way possible. It was hard at first, but by the end I was dancing like a fool. Since then, when I'm feeling pissed off or worried about a trade, I'll get up from my desk and dance ridiculously. A passer-by might indeed think I looked psycho. The nerd dancing might be especially good for male traders who are battling the big ego. If your ego won't let you look that stupid, there are plenty of more conventional physical outlets for trade rage.

# Trading tip no. 13

## Overbought signals

When a stock or market is overbought, it is at risk of a correction. Keeping this important fact in mind should help you keep your trailing stop procedure tight and discourage you from acting on weak or late entry signals. While there are specific technical indicators that give overbought and oversold signals, I like to study the pure price action, because it's primary information and the only thing that really matters. Note the spot gold chart below. Drawing simple trendlines under the price action makes acceleration in the gains become obvious. The rally in gold from late August to 22 September showed an accelerated upward movement to the peak. This was followed by a sideways correction that lasted for more than three weeks.

© IT-Finance

# Week 14

## Out with a bang

## Day 65

Monday, 26 September
Total: $28,351, US$970

---

Last night I had dinner with friends of mine, a couple. The husband has his own hedge fund. He helped me get my first broking job in Sydney when I got back from living in London in 1997. Later I introduced him to his wife and now they have two children.

I discussed the excellent workmanship of fake designer handbags in Hong Kong with the wife, and the strategy of keeping a short portfolio of dog ASX stocks as a hedge against long positions in high-momentum stocks with the husband. High-momentum stocks are stocks that can trend strongly. The strategy is otherwise known as a 'pairs trade', and it involves taking a long position in one share CFD and a short position of equal value in another. The idea is to make money from the relative moves and be hedged against a big move in either direction on the market. My friend's strategy is to take a series of short positions in the worst performing stocks in the worst performing sectors over the long-term.

There are a few key stocks in the index that have been sitting in the kennel for a matter of months and even years. Some of these might eventually go off the board; that is, be de-listed. What happens then, I wonder. Back to The Director, who tells me that for share traders who have long positions, the consequences of de-listing are straightforward – they lose all their money, unless there is anything left to be distributed to shareholders, which there usually isn't.

The situation for CFD traders is different. Typically, they will be asked to fully fund their accounts. For example, imagine that you are long 10,000 share CFDs in stock XYZ and the company is trading at $1 when it goes off the board. If you are currently funding your position with a margin (say $500 or $1000), you will have to fund the whole $10,000. The position is no longer on margin. The same applies to short positions. If you don't have $10,000, you may be closed out of your short position at the last traded price. When a company goes bust, the chances are that nothing will be returned to shareholders, so, as a short seller, you will most likely receive the full $10,000 plus your deposit back. The problem is that these issues can take years to resolve, and the CFD provider cannot pay out on short positions until there is an official ruling by the liquidators.

To avoid the situation of a stock going off the board altogether and the associated administrative problems which follow, it would be wise, when the next bear market comes, to take profits on winning short positions periodically. With CFDs, the transaction costs are low, so jumping in and out of the market every few months or weeks could be a relatively inexpensive insurance policy.

# Day 66

Tuesday, 27 September
Total: $28,626, US$802

---

I spend the entire session on a plane to Perth and lose a trading day. I arrive at 4.00 pm, just as the market is closing. My markets pager, which has been off the air while I'm in the sky, kicks in when I land, but without charts I feel like I'm running blind. I go to an internet cafe and check the damage on the charts. I notice that I've given back a heap of profit on a position in Hardman Resources (HDR) after it made new highs today. Because I couldn't watch the price action today, I wasn't able to trail my stop-loss, which is my usual exit style.

I'm trying to plan ahead now, before I have to get back on the plane tomorrow. I'll have a window of half an hour before the plane takes off, enough time to wait for opening action and make a few prudent exits.

# Day 67

Wednesday, 28 September
Total: $27,973, US$1124

---

At the airport, I am frantically checking my pager as the market opens when I learn that the plane is delayed. It is the first time I'm grateful for a plane delay. I have an extra half an hour to manage my open positions. The first thing I notice as the market opens is that BSL gaps down a massive 40¢. I haven't seen this coming, but it's through my stop so I must be closed out on the open. I'm watching the action on my pager.

Flying across country and trading don't mix. Trading for a living has given me less free time than I ever had as a freelance journalist/analyst and has chained me to my desk. Sick days – forget about them. With my style of trading, I always have open positions, and they need to be managed even if I have a hangover or the flu. If you're sick enough, it's probably wise to close everything out until you feel better. One more thing I've learned: don't try to manage short-term trades while you're on holiday. It's best to close out and go away with no open positions. Otherwise, it's not much of a holiday, and it will probably cost you more than you anticipated. Of course, this depends on your trading style. If you have a longer term outlook, or base your analysis on end-of-day data, you can afford to be away from the price action and not risk losing money, as long as you are placing stop and contingent orders.

Later in the day I discover that BSL gapped down because the stock was going ex-dividend. I've made back in dividends everything I lost on the trade and more. The money will be credited to my account tonight. CFDs mean there is no hassle waiting for dividend cheques.

# Day 68

Thursday, 29 September
Total: $28,284, US$1289

---

A friend sends me an article today which includes comments made by Stephen Roach, Morgan Stanley's famous chief economist. He thinks that the retirement of the current US Fed Chairman Alan Greenspan early in 2006 might trigger a meltdown in one or other of the financial markets in the US. According to Roach, the changeover of Fed Chairman in the past has been followed by big corrections in the US. This might be the trigger event Noland is expecting. I'll be staying tuned for that.

I get a call from one of the InvestorWeb members who saw me speak at the Sydney seminar last week. After we talk about the mechanics of placing stop orders, he asks me the big question. 'I want to quit my job and start trading CFDs for a living. Do you have any advice?'

It's the dream of nearly everyone who gets involved in trading. It's also one of the most challenging career paths you can chose. No career with this much upside comes easily. You can make or lose thousands of dollars in seconds, so it takes more than just a good trading approach to get you through. You must be emotionally fit for the challenge, willing to persevere even when the losses are mounting and have the absolute belief that it is possible to make a living from trading. Give yourself a trading education: read as many books on the subject as you can, talk to successful traders, find a coach and get therapy if you think you have some lurking emotional issues.

# Day 69

Friday, 30 September
Total: $28,824, US$1091

---

Today is the last day of my trading diary. My goal was to finish on a high. I go out with a bang, booking profits in six trades out of eight. The biggest is in Caltex (CTX); I make $1400 on a small position of 1000 share CFDs. I also clock some good profits in Paladin Resources (PDN), making money on two out of three pyramided positions. I withdraw $2000 today, bringing the total debits from my account since I started making money to $14,000. This equates to $1000 a week for the duration of the book, although I didn't withdraw the first $1000 until I'd been keeping the diary for more than a month. I leave eleven positions open. My balance as at close of today is $30,257, consisting of: $14,824; plus $1433 (my US dollar balance converted to Australian dollars); and $14,000 in funds withdrawn from my account. This is my largest balance since I started the book.

I take three of my back-tested system trades out today because the moving average crossover has turned down. My net profit on them is $2002. The first trade was placed in early September, so I've achieved a 20% return in just a month: not a bad result. These trades were also single trades. I didn't pyramid positions or pre-empt exit signals by trailing stop-loss orders. This successful experiment demonstrates the value of a low maintenance trading system for traders who are not able to monitor prices on an intra-day basis. Such a system would enable part-time traders to get their feet wet without taking the plunge into a full-time trading career. Any system developed on end-of-day data would be a great way for new traders to start trading without needing to give up their day jobs.

I'm speaking to a large-scale trader I know from Queensland. He is in town to present a seminar. He is a short-term trader – intra-day or a couple of days max. I ask him what is happening with his trading while he is away from his office. He tells me he has closed everything out and has no positions. I think this is the best thing to do when you cannot properly monitor the market. If I had been in a losing streak when the week started, I might have been tempted to cut everything, but with so many winners I decided to wing it. It has worked this time, but I don't think it's good practice.

## The story at the end of this diary
----------------------------------------
Profit/Loss to date – $15,824 profit

## This week

Closed positions – 21; Open positions – 11
Winners – 13; Losers – 8; Win/loss ratio – 0.62
Biggest loss – $670; Biggest win – $1,471
Number of consecutive losing trades – 2

I'm always surprised that I manage at least one loss a week that goes well beyond my $350 risk limit. Despite this, I can't complain about my overall result.

## What have I learnt?

- Despite the current bull market, a portfolio of short positions is a smart move if you can find stocks that show long-term weakness and have low volatility. These have the advantage of paying interest to my account. Worked with stop-loss orders, they can provide another stream of profit. The challenge is finding the right stocks when the market is as strong as it is now.

## Do's and don'ts

- Do be aware of important news, even if you are a technical trader like me. I read a lot of material from more fundamental commentators and am interested in anyone who has an opinion that is not mainstream. Being open to opinions and aware of critical events such as the Fed Chairman change or even geo-political events can affect your trading outcomes.

- Do watch for potential short positions, no matter what the general outlook.

- Don't leave short-term positions open when you are on holiday or unable to monitor your trades with your usual dedication.

# Lingo and lessons

## Margin calculations for spot gold CFD position: Australian and US dollar requirement

Trading gold from Australia in US dollars means you have currency exposure, so there are effectively two deposits taken from your account to cover margin. One is in US dollars and one is in Australian dollars. The total amount will be 1% of the total exposure.

## Pairs trading

Some traders make a living just from pairs trading. A few years ago I interviewed a couple of would-be hedge fund managers who were pairs trading CFDs across different exchanges. This kind of strategy would work in present circumstances if you went long, say, Australian resource shares, and short US resource shares, thinking that local resource shares will outperform US resource companies. My CFD provider's platform allows you to do both from the same platform with no extra costs and without the conversion of funds into foreign currency. The idea of pairs trading is to find stocks or sectors that have demonstrated historical price correlation. This relationship will either narrow or widen. The idea is to enter the pairs trade when the price differential is at one of these extremes.

# Trading tip no. 14
## Simple shorting signal

The traditional rule for shorting is to pick the weakest stock in the weakest sector. Another way to find shorting opportunities is to watch for underperformers on strongly bullish days. If the local index is rallying, say, 30 points and above, and a particular stock, without any news announcement, goes lower, it should be on your shorting watch list. In a bull market, the dead cat bounce of a weak stock can be steep and hit obvious stop-loss levels before going lower again. A favourite sell signal of mine is a test and subsequent rejection of old highs intra-day. I then sell at the first retracement and break of support. This signal might be in the form of a double top pattern formed intra-day or a break of the previous day's support at the close. On the HDR daily chart below, the price retested old highs and then proceeded to form a double top pattern on two occasions.

© IT-Finance

# Postscript

Five days after the final trading day covered in this book, the S&P/ASX 200 dropped around 100 points a day on two days in a row. Luckily I had very few long positions and had taken some tentative short positions, which I continued to build on as the market fell. The ability to go from long to short as the market unfolds into the downside is vital for a short-term trader. The fact that it was as easy as taking a long position was crucial to my success at that time. CFDs offer a simple, cheap and efficient means of exploiting downside price action.

# Hindsight: Can you make money trading CFDs?

Before I started this trading diary, The Director told me that the most common questions he is asked by clients are 'Can you make money from trading CFDs?' and 'How do you do it?'

To prove that CFDs can be traded profitably, I could have bought the Aussie 200 index CFD on day one of the book and sold it on the last day. In a bull market anyone can make money. Back when I was a futures broker, a new client proudly explained to me his great trading track record. This was back in the late 1990s, and his self-belief was based on one thing – he had subscribed to Telstra Corporation in the float and held the shares. If he is still holding those shares, he has given back most of that profit by now. A successful trader is not someone who takes a few lucky positions in a rising market. A good trader profits in rising or falling markets, cuts losses, pyramids positions for exponential gains and knows how to keep losses to a minimum when the market gets choppy. If you feel you are a 'lucky' trader, it's likely that you've just caught the best part of a bull market. A real trader knows that luck has nothing to do with success.

Nevertheless, I believe that anyone can make money trading CFDs. Not only can it be done, but it is possible to do it in a style that does not fit the stereotype of the hard-core Wall Street–style trader. I am often undisciplined; occasionally ego-driven; a procrastinator; a person who thinks a vomiting dog can predict the market; and I find wisdom in cable-TV dating shows. Despite this, I still traded CFDs very profitably. The conclusion I want you to draw here is that CFD trading is not prohibitively difficult. It takes patience and confidence and perseverance, but it does not require any special skills that cannot be acquired through learning and practice.

My win/loss ratio was less than 50%, which means the number of losing trades was higher than the number of winning trades. These figures clearly demonstrate that I have no special gift for predicting the market in the short-term. In fact, the trading diary showed me that I regularly resolved to improve certain aspects of my trading only to fall back into bad habits that were instinctive. I didn't always learn from my mistakes.

The other day a friend of mine said to me, 'Shit happens and then you forget about it.' Aldous Huxley was responsible for the highbrow version of this saying: 'That men do not learn very much from the lessons of history is the most important of all the lessons of history.' I believe this saying sums up the markets and trading better than any other. It certainly applies to the merry-go-round of bull and bear markets: when the market is soaring, we are quick to forget that ups and downs are par for the course. The saying also gives us insight into why the market is run entirely by human emotions, and not the rational intellect of central bankers or economists. If it was logical the 'shit' wouldn't keep happening in the markets. Huxley's words also highlight why we repeat the same mistakes so many times. Our responses are driven by short-term feelings and not by a patient, long-term, disciplined plan. It reminds me that the path to trading mastery is ongoing and never ending.

## My stats

Having logged every trade on a spreadsheet, I have been able to break down the figures, gaining some interesting insights into which stocks I traded best and worst and which stocks I should probably stop trading altogether. Here are the highlights:

## Aristocrat Leisure (ALL)

I traded Aristocrat Leisure (ALL) a total of 25 times. My biggest single win on ALL was my biggest win on a single position for all trades: $2516 after brokerage and financing charges. My single biggest loss was $449 after brokerage. I had 15 losing trades and 10 winning trades. My net profit and loss on this stock was $2297, which means if I'd taken out the one big winner, I would have made a net loss trading this stock.

## BlueScope Steel (BSL)

I took 29 trades on BSL. My biggest win was only $619, while my largest loss was $526. Given how confident I was about trading this stock, I managed to end in the red with a net loss of $1138.

## Excel Coal (EXL)

Excel Coal (EXL) was my second biggest winner. My total net profit on it was a lovely $6135. My biggest loss was $445 and the biggest win was $1532.

## Jubilee Mines (JBM)

If I hadn't suffered one huge loss on Jubilee Mines (JBM), I would have made a small net loss trading this stock. Instead the net figure was a loss of $1405.

## Newcrest Mining (NCM)

I had a return of $2978 on Newcrest Mining (NCM), from a total of 35 trades. My biggest loser was $509 and biggest winner was $1469.

### Oxiana (OXR)

Oxiana (OXR) was my quiet achiever. I only took six trades on this stock and lost on only one. The loss was just $377, and the biggest win was $1471, giving me a net profit on this stock of $4061.

### Paladin (PDN)

Considering I had no idea what Paladin (PDN) did before someone alerted me to uranium stocks, my net return on this stock was fabulous: $7035 from just 16 trades. My biggest win was $1772 on 7000 lots and my biggest loss was $377 on the same amount. I only had three losing trades on PDN.

### Ventracor (VCR)

Ventracor (VCR) is my personal dog. I traded it nine times for only one profitable trade of a measly $212. The biggest loss was $610. My net loss $2185.

\* \* \*

Another interesting way to weigh up my trading results is to compare my local market returns to those of the S&P/ASX 200 index. Between 28 June and 30 September (the date on which I finished the diary), the index gained just over 9.6%. Annualised, this is an impressive return of over 38% per annum. However, it seems paltry when compared with my returns over the three-month trading period of more than 121%. The graph on page 218 at the end of this final chapter makes this very obvious.

## Keep it simple

It is possible to have a simple trading style with CFDs because CFDs themselves are very simple. As I stated at the outset, there is no other retail share-derivative product that allows you to trade the same price levels as shares, with the same scale of price movement versus underlying value, and still benefit from leverage. I believe the simplicity of the product has helped it become a retail trading revolution.

The simplicity of the product is matched by the simplicity of my approach. You'll notice that I haven't supplied any sophisticated mathematical formulas in this book. This was not a deliberate decision – it was just a consequence of my methods. New traders who picked up this book looking for a black and white, indicator-based strategy might have found this frustrating: all I do is trade with the trend, monitoring support and resistance. Perhaps the most important thing to know about trading is that your actual strategy for buying and selling is something that evolves through personal experience.

The trading tips I have supplied at the end of each chapter are based on real-life trading observations which I have converted into strategies that I use on a regular basis. None of them are complicated or require any special mathematical skills or mastery. Try them out and see if they suit your trading style and are applicable to the charts you trade.

I am hoping these tips may be of some assistance as you develop your own trading style.

Always remember, though, that markets are dynamic. An observation that was true or a strategy that worked a year ago might not in a year's time. Stocks change their character as time goes on, too. Keep this in mind when the next bear market hits. To be a successful trader you must continually evolve and refine your strategy. I expect that in five or ten years time my trading style will still contain some of the elements detailed in the strategies of this book, but I hope that I will also have incorporated many new smarter insights on the market into my overall approach.

If you already have an approach you are happy with, I urge you to work on improving your money management techniques, such as using stop-loss orders and scaling into positions to amplify returns.

Another means of keeping your CFD trading simple is to use the back-testing system facility on your trading platform. These facilities allow would-be traders who are testing the waters to place a small amount of money on the line and watch a trading system in action. They provide useful information about the behaviour of technical indicators, such as the amount of slippage you may encounter after receiving an entry or exit signal and how long after the initial reversal of a trend you should wait before entering or exiting a trade. These are important considerations when you are trading a technical indicator–based system. I would recommend that anyone who wants to start trading and has never traded before should run a back-tested system on a wide number of share CFDs at the same time, taking small trades in a limited amount of share CFDs. The combination of paper and real-life trading is the best preparation for scaling up to more professional trading in which you risk serious money.

## Emotional mastery

For me, the constant challenge in the trading process was not getting to grips with a particular stock or with the markets, but overcoming my instinctive emotional responses. Trading demands a complete disregard for popular opinion, reigning exuberance, general pessimism and the advice of so-called experts. It is truly the journey of the lone wolf. When you trade, it really is you against the world. I found it helped to have a trading coach, but if you are new to the game, your first step should be a trading course, one that offers the chance to talk to teachers who have traded or who are trading still.

## Finding a coach or mentor

My trading coach is like a bird on my shoulder. I am often sitting in front of my screen, contemplating what to do about a trade, when one of his sayings comes into my head. It has helped me to get back into winning trades when I've cut too early and to scratch non-performing trades at the end of the day rather than holding them overnight and risking a loss. At least once in every session my trading coach says to me that he has faith in me and now I think I finally believe it. He understands and supports me and makes the worst days feel like a normal part of the trading process. You can't ask for more than this when you enter Waterworld. Having a trading coach is about the only thing that lessens the feelings of loneliness on this journey.

## Getting therapy or counselling

My hypnotherapist also helped me. She used two other techniques apart from the hypnotherapy: neuro-linguistic programming (NLP) and some straight counselling. All three seemed to work. During the hypno sessions I sometimes felt like I was faking it, that I wasn't really going under, but I always felt better afterwards, so I think they worked despite my cynicism. Only one session was directly related to money. We discovered I didn't like receiving money from my parents as a child because I felt disapproved of for asking. This carried over into my trading – I didn't feel I deserved big profits.

My emotional outlook lifted dramatically the week I started receiving hypnotherapy as well as having face-to-face sessions with my trading coach. It took longer for the big turnaround to manifest in my profits. There's something to be said for caring for the psyche. Don't immediately blame your trading system if you start making a series of losses. Your problem may be as simple as an upbringing that instilled in you the common belief that money only comes from hard work. Trading for a living blows that away.

215

## Getting smart

This book enabled me to learn a few important lessons. The first is that a bad habit is hard to break even when the negative consequences of that bad habit are staring you in the face. I constantly lost money by adding to positions prematurely, and could see that my scaling-in approach needed to be improved. Despite this, I persisted with this behaviour and continued to add too early. Of course I always felt vindicated when the scaling-in resulted in a very profitable position.

Another lesson reinforced by the process of writing the book was the importance of stop-loss orders and the need to be more scrupulous with them. I often went to market automatically in my usual trade size, without considering the stop-loss order level. When I determined the stop-loss level after I had already placed the order, I often found a larger stop-loss level was required and this meant I rarely kept to my limit of $350. This problem was highlighted when I looked at the results stock by stock. Not surprisingly, despite some good pyramiding of positions across the board, the largest total returns I made were on the stocks I traded with the smallest losses, usually around my limit of $350.

## Method in the madness

Two things set my trading style apart from that of the amateur trader:

1. my use of stop-loss orders

2. my willingness to scale in or pyramid positions.

Neither of these two aspects of my trading could have been successfully carried out to the same effect in the traditional sharemarket.

Even within the CFD market, you will find that not all CFD providers offer real protection via stop-loss orders. With some CFD providers, your stop-loss level acts as a trigger and this becomes a limit order, which means it may not be filled. This is the same way a stop order is executed in the share market. This is potentially very dangerous and defeats the purpose of trading with stops. It also means you cannot safely walk away from the trading platform, but must stay vigilant for stops that may not be filled. I would suggest that before establishing a CFD account with a new provider, you should ask about the exact procedure followed in executing stop-loss orders. If a stop order can potentially become a limit order, I would search for another provider.

Pyramiding into positions is possible in the traditional share market, but requires more capital outlay. In the CFD market, scaling-in is an efficient and smart use of the expanding capital that results from a profitable position.

## My most important lesson

The most important lesson I learned from the experience of trading and writing this book was that I have the ability to return from and prosper after defeat. Every CFD trader will lose at some stage. Some losses force you to change your strategy, while others urge you to change the whole way you think. The longer you've been in the business, the more likely it will be the latter.

If you decide to trade seriously, I think you'll find it will change you as a person. Don't underestimate the gravity of the task. If you are successful in the long-term, you truly have found your character.

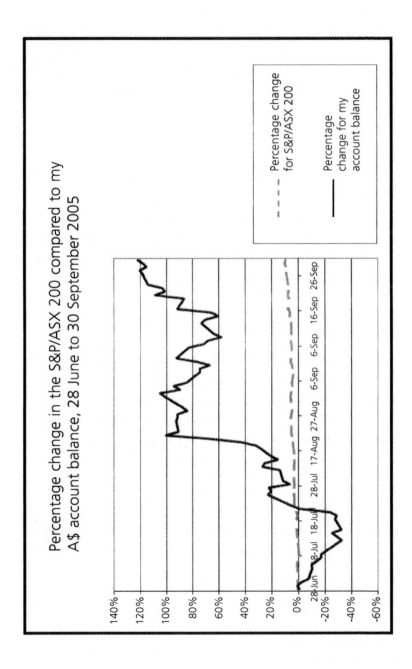

Percentage change in the S&P/ASX 200 compared to my A$ account balance, 28 June to 30 September 2005

# Index

# U

# V

# W